TUSCANY

Its History, Art and Natural Beauty

editions **ITALCARDS** bologna - italy

A Brief History

Time-honoured wellspring of glorious traditions, soil which nurtured a civilisation that was to leave an indelible mark on the development of the peoples of ancient Italy, a history spanning 3000 years the events of which have always been bonded together by a common thread — the will to forge and preserve a unity of spirit, language, culture and art even in the face of the most trying adversity, even in times when its very independence had been lost. Tuscany.

That history was given new impetus sometime after 1000 B.C. by the Etruscans (see p. 154 where they are discussed at length), who settled the area bounded by the Arno and Tiber rivers and the Tyrrhenian Sea. They were called Tyrsenes or Tyrrhenoi by the Greeks and Etruschi or Turci by the Romans — whence the name Etruria or Tuscia for the region they inhabited. The modern term Toscana, or Tuscany, owes its origin to the rise and spread of «vulgar» Italian as the common language in the 12-13th centuries. They found that nature had been generous. The area was endowed with a mild, agreeable climate, wooded mountains, arable hillsides, fertile lowlands, ore deposits, and an extensive coastline along which flourished a thriving trade with the East.

The Etruscans were innovators. They were the first people in Italy to organise their society within a political and institutional framework. Although they did not develop a united, centralised form of government, their common religious, cultural and national identity provided the cohesive foundations upon which the independent Etruscan city-states, a system similar to the Greek polis, established their coexistence, despite the inevitable rivalries and skirmishes amongst them. This sense of purpose was also evident in the economic sphere where the Etruscans were the first to apply rational and systematic criteria to the exploitation of their natural resources.

At the height of its power and splendour (7th-6th centuries B.C.), Etruria had expanded both north and south of its original territory by conquest, bringing under its rule part of Latium — Rome itself was governed for more than a century by the Tarquinians, Etruscan kings — Campania, Umbria, and into the Po valley and Corsica. Its hegemony on land and sea rivalled that of the Greeks and Phoenicians. By the 5th century B.C., however, decline had set in and the slow yet inexorable end begun.

The Etruscans were unable to stem, first, the expansionist designs along the Tyrrhenian coast of the Greeks and Carthaginians and, later, the unrelenting territorial pressures from the Italic peoples, the Gauls and the Romans. The Etruscans gradually gave ground, retreating into their own territories. The most serious, and increasingly the most menacing, challenge to their power was the rise of Rome which, by military might and the power of persuasion brought to bear on those cities linked by friendship to it, succeeded in dominating all of Etruria from the 4th to the 3rd centuries B.C.

Rome conceded the newly conquered cities a certain degree of administrative autonomy, although the former Etruria would become under Augustus' reorganisation of the Empire Region VII. Despite its romanisation, Etruscan unity remained largely intact thanks to the cohesive nature of the underlying political, cultural and religious forces.

Roman rule was later to be replaced by the barbarian reign of the Goths and Alamanni (5th century A.D.), harbingers of war and destruction heralding the inevitable decline of Tuscany's cities and its cultural and civic traditions. Following the successive wave of invasion and subsequent settlement by the Langobards under the banner of feudalism in the 6th century A.D., the region regained its political unity by establishing the Marquisate of Tuscany with its administrative capital at Lucca. With the rise of the communes in the 11th and 12th centuries, and the new towns, autonomous cities and independent states the new order brought into being, Tuscany succeeded by dint of its strong cultural and spiritual traditions in retaining its unity in art and language.

This is a period of new social forces, forces of vision calling forth an innovative will to shape a new political and administrative order in the life of these cities. Renewed enterprise in trade and manufacturing represents the cornerstone of reinvigorated economy. Pisa is the first to scale the heights of power and prestige. Linked to the sea by its harbour, it soon extends its hegemony over the entire region, a position of preeminence it was not to relinquish for a long time. It is Florence that next steps upon the stage, supplanting Pisa as the arbiter of power in Tuscany.

Ever astute politically, Florence had laid the groundwork of its policies in the early 1300s. With single-minded purpose, it set about to shape the disparate elements of Tuscany into a united self-governing state with itself as the seat of that government. By 1400 Florentine supremacy was unchallenged, a success due as much to the city's contribution to the cultural and artistic renewal as to the rise of the Signoria of the Medici family and their new political order which was to supplant the old communes.

Supremacy, however, was not necessarily unification, and it was not until 1532 and the treaty between Pope Clement VII and Charles V that the region achieved the political cohesiveness enabling it to become a unified, regional state. A brief period of decline typified by the

Camping Italia nearby Torre del Lago.

Toscana

Emilia
Romagna

Liguria

MAR TIRRENO

Lazio

Umbria

Marche

Pontremoli · la Cisa
CARRARA
MASSA
Barga
Bagni di Lucca
Forte dei Marmi
Viareggio
Lago Trasimeno
PISA
LUCCA
Collodi
Vinci
Abetone · M. Cimone (2165)
Corno alle Scale
PISTOIA
Prato
Certeto Guidi
Montecatini T.
Empoli
Certaldo
S. Geminiano
Volterra
Cecina
Arno
Futa
Vicchio
Fiesole
Portassieve
FIRENZE
Vallombrosa
M. Falterona (1654)
Eremo di Camaldoli
Poppi
La Verna
M. Fumaiolo (1407)
Caprese Michelangelo
Sansepolcro
AREZZO
Cortona
CHIANTI
SIENA
Monte Oliveto Maggiore
I. Gorgogna
I. Capraia
Populonia
Piombino
Portoferraio
I. d'Elba
Punta Ala
Castiglione della Pescaia
Marina di Grosseto
I. del Giglio
I. Montecristo
Massa Marittima
Follonica
Le Colline Metallifere
Roccastrada
Montalcino
Pienza
Chianciano
Chiusi
M. Amiata (1734)
Ombrone
GROSSETO
Sovana
M. Argentario
Orbatello
Alpi Apuane

Tuscan landscape in winter

weak stewardship of Cosimo II and Ferdinand II, with the latter's rule marking the ultimate physical and moral demise of the Medicis, was followed by the economic and political recovery of the Grand Duchy under the leadership of the Lorenas (18th century), who completed the region's unification. Their impact was felt in all phases of endeavour, from the suppression of many feudal privileges and the formation of liberal economic policies to the promotion of agriculture through land reclamation and the granting of greater political autonomy to the communes.

Throughout Italy, meanwhile, political ferment, which would culminate in the Risorgimento or unification of Italy, was reaching fever pitch. Tuscany and Florence, in particular, became by virtue of their cultural and civic example the banner and spiritual symbol rallying all Italians who would fight for a new, politically united Italy.

The annexation to the Kingdom of Sardinia took place in 1860, while, from 1865 to 1871, Florence was the capital of Italy. The development of a workers' and socialist movement began to gain momentum towards the end of the century and organise on a more solid footing after 1900.

With its numerous partisan units and the support of the population, Tuscany contributed much to the struggle for liberation during World War II, one example of which was the popular insurrection in the summer of 1944 that forced the fascists and German troops to retreat. In the aftermath of the world conflict, Tuscany, having chosen to heal the social wounds and reconstruct the material damage incurred by its cities and towns in a spirit of reconciliation, succeeded in re-entering the national mainstream as one of the leading regions in the country.

☆ ☆ ☆

Perhaps no other Italian region can boast such a wealth of natural and artistic treasures as Tuscany. Sea, Alps and Apennines, verdant pine woods, natural parks and rolling hills; a climate favoured by the combination of various factors which make for short winters and a long spring; famous thermal resorts and winter sports centres; and agricultural produce that is envied the world over: what could be added to complete such a list? Alongside these natural treasures, there is the art and architecture: not locked away in museums, but there for all to see, basking in the sun in the towns and cities, and in the villages scattered along the Valdarno, the Val d'Elsa... So great is the artistic wealth of Tuscany that it is difficult to know where to begin. Should we start with Florence or Pisa? Arezzo or Siena? Livorno or Lucca? And then Grosseto, Massa Carrara and Pistoia? Or Prato, Volterra, Cortona, San Miniato, San Gimignano, Sansepolcro, Pescia, Anghiari... The list could go on for ever, for even the smallest villages boast precious art treasures which tell of a glorious past. And not only the distant past was glorious: the more recent past, too, has left us its own lasting monuments. For if Florence was the capital of Italy only for a limited period, Tuscany has always been the capital of Italian art; it is here that Italian art — like the Italian language — finds its true roots.

Tuscany is not just a region to visit, but one to «experience» over a period of time. Its economy is primarily agricultural (one has only to think of the vineyards from which come the magnificent wines of Chianti, of Elba and of Montepulciano, or the olive trees which provide such highly-prized oil), but it does not lack other sources of income. Rich in mineral resources (iron ore from the island of Elba, mercury from Monte Amiata, marble from the Apuan Alps, lignite from the Valdarno, etc.), it also has the industries to work them. And, alongside these, there are the various, traditional craft industries: leather goods, straw-work, embroidery, glassware, ceramics, alabaster, metals, wood, cloth: in short, nothing is lacking.

Also worthy of mention is Tuscan cuisine: good, plain, wholesome cooking based on roast meats, game and fish, dressed with the exquisite oil and accompanied by excellent wines. And there are also the many sweet specialities, such as the biscuits of Prato, «cantucci», castagnacci, panforti, buccellato, «cenci», zuccotti, etc.

Finally we should mention the folklore, to be found in great abundance throughout the whole of Tuscany. Take, for example, the «Palio» of Siena, watched enthusiastically every year by tens of thousands of people when it takes place on 2nd July and 16th August. Every city, town and village, practically, has its own special annual festival linked to its traditions and to its history. At Arezzo there is the Tournament of the Saracen and at Pistoia that of the Bear; at Lucca the Festival of the Crossbow; at Pisa the Battle of the Bridges and the Regatta of the Marine Republics; at San Sepolcro the Festival of the Crossbowmen; at Grosseto the Rose Tournament... And then there are the many Florentine festivals — the historical football match in period costume, the «scoppio del carro» (the blowing up of a float), the festival of the cricket, the paper lantern festival, etc. — and those of more recent institution, such as the Carnival of Viareggio.

As far as cultural activities are concerned, we must not forget the famous «Maggio Musicale Fiorentino» — the Florentine May Music Festival — and the numerous exhibitions of art, antiques, crafts, cinema and literature which make of Tuscany a forge in which the fire never dies.

FLORENCE

History

The earliest traces of civilization in the Arno valley date back to the Iron Age. The area was for many centuries under Etruscan dominion, until it was conquered by the Romans who founded a «Municipium» known as «Florentia».

Despite the ravages of the subsequent invasions suffered by the colony, it nevertheless managed to achieve a remarkable degree of prosperity towards the end of the X century, the period which saw the construction of the Baptistry, the first architectural masterpiece of the city.

In the centuries that followed, Florence became the cradle of the Renaissance and the centre of European civilization, thanks in part to its increasing economic power and in part to the intellectual and political capacities of its leading citizens, qualities that have characterized the city through the centuries.

Ruled over, at first, by the Marquises of Tuscany, it was later to become the scene of violent struggles between this ancient, noble family and the increasingly powerful guilds of craftsmen. Out of this deep rivalry two opposing factions were formed: the «Guelfi», partisans of the Pope, and the «Ghibellini», partisans of the Emperor.

These internal struggles did not, however, prevent the exceptional cultural, political and economic development of Florence which, by the end of the XIII century, had succeeded in spreading its dominion over the cities of Arezzo, Pistoia and Siena. This was the period that witnessed the flowering of the genius of the artists Giotto, Cimabue and Arnolfo di Cambio and of the great poet Dante, while the following century saw the literary masterpieces of Petrarca and Boccaccio and the architectural ones of Andrea di Cione, known as «Orcagna».

On the political front, the XIV century saw the so-called «Tumulto dei Ciompi» (1378), a rebellion of the lowest working classes against the richer middle class, after which the Medici Family began, under Cosimo the Elder, to assert and expand its influence: from this time on, the Medici would rule over Florence for almost three centuries.

Cosimo was succeeded by his son Piero, but it was under Lorenzo, named «Il Magnifico», Cosimo's grandson, patron of the arts, himself an artist and outstanding politician, that Florence reached the height of its splendour.

The most important artists of this period include Brunelleschi, Michelozzo, Masaccio, Beato Angelico, Paolo Uccello, Filippo Lippi, Botticelli and Donatello, a list which culminates in the two greater figures of Renaissance art: Leonardo and Michelangelo.

After the death of Lorenzo, the Republicans, who had always been hostile to the Medici, instigated by the Dominican friar Girolamo Savonarola, seemed to gain the upper hand, but the Medici returned to power once more and ruled until 1737 when the last of the Medici dynasty, Gian Gastone, died.

Once annexed to the Kingdom of Italy, it served as the capital from 1865 to 1871. With the advent of the unification of Italy, the workers' movement began to gain momentum through such associations as the «Società di Mutuo Soccorso» (Mutual Aid Society) and the «Fratellanza Artigiana» (Brotherhood of Artisans) which would lead to the formation of a strong democratic political force and the socialist movement. Following the wide-spread destruction caused by the German troops during the Second World War, the city rebelled in August 1944 against its occupiers, an insurrection that helped to secure its liberation and facilitate the advance of the allied armies.

Florence was devastated by flood in November 1966 and its works of art were seriously damaged. With tenacity, expertise and pride, the city was able to restore and recover almost everything.

Today Florence is a fine city spread out along the banks of the River Arno, surrounded by fertile hills covered with vineyards, orchards and olive groves.

Industry, commerce and handicrafts all flourish, but it is above all as a centre of culture that Florence is recognized the world over. As well as the University, the Cherubini Academy of Music, the museums and the churches, there are many magnificent, ancient palaces in which concerts, plays and exhibitions are held regularly: the Florentine calendar is full of artistic and cultural events of all kinds which draw people from all over the world.

Football in costume.

PIAZZA DEL DUOMO

LOGGIA DEL BIGALLO

Built on Gothic Florentine architectural structures, it is ascribed to Alberto Arnoldi (1352-1358) and stands in front of the south door of the Baptistry.

Originally it housed the «Confraternita della Misericordia» which used to show abandoned children to public charity; then it went to the «Compagnia ospedaliera del Bigallo».

On the side facing the square one can admire the statues of «St. Lucy», the «Virgin» and «St. Peter, martyr», of the school of Nino Pisano; at a lower level, in the lunette of the door, there is the «Madonna with Child», by Arnoldi (1361).

THE DUOMO (S. MARIA DEL FIORE)

Begun in 1296 by Arnolfo di Cambio on the site of the old Cathedral of St. Reparata, work was interrupted when he died (1310). After various vicissitudes the project was resumed on a much grander scale in 1357 by Francesco Talenti, who designed the great pillars. The vault of the central nave was finished in 1378, and by 1421 work had reached the drum of the dome. The dome itself was built by Brunelleschi between 1420 and 1436, after his daring and controversial project had been accepted, but the lantern and ball that surmount it were not completed until as late as 1461.

Loggia del Bigallo.

Duomo, Baptistry and Bell Tower.

Panorama and Santa Maria del Fiore Cathedral.

Cathedral Interior. *Michelangelo: The Pietà.* ▶

THE FAÇADE: The original façade remained unfinished (it was adorned with many statues most of which are now kept in the Museum of the Opera del Duomo), and was demolished in 1587. The present façade was built on a design by Emilio De Fabris and finished in 1887. However, in spite of the praise-worthy attempt to retrace the original motives of the sides and the apse, the façade does not entirely fit in with the ensemble of the building, for lack of authentic stylistic inspiration, even though it has a certain dignity of its own. Of the three bronze doors the left one (1897) and the central one (1903) are the work of A. Passaglia, the right one (1899) of G. Cassioli. The statues and the mosaics on the façade were made between the end of the XIX and the beginning of the XX century.

In the square in front of the church every year, at Easter, the traditional and famous explosion of the «Carro» takes place, after a dove has flown from the altar inside the Duomo to the Baptistry.

THE SIDES AND THE APSES: In the first and oldest section of the right side, between close pillars, there is the «Porta del Campanile», dating from the second half of the XIV century. Further ahead, between two big mullioned windows, there is the «Porta dei Canonici» in late-Gothic style, dating from the end of the XIV and the beginning of the XV century. Then, round the enormous bulk of the apses supporting the drum of the dome, with three big poligonal niches and two smaller ones with elegant Gothic mullioned windows, one reaches the north side of the Cathedral, identical to the south side, where there is the «Porta della Mandorla». In Gothic-Renaissance style, it dates from the beginning of the XV century and is certainly the most important one for its architectural elegance and the richness of its ornaments. Above it there is the «Assunta» a relief by Nanni di Banco (1414-21), framed in a «mandorla» (almond). On the side pinnacles there are two «Statuettes of Prophets», ascribed to

young Donatello and, in the lunette, a mosaic by the Ghirlandaio family. Then there is the «Porta della Balla», late XIV century.

THE INTERIOR: In the shape of a latin cross, it is divided into three aisles by polistyle pilasters, with high arches and ogival vaults giving it great elegance, while the vast spaces of the Gothic style induce a sense of severe magnificence. On the inside of the façade and in the aisles there are, among many others, works by Ghiberti (stained-glass windows), Tino di Camaino, Benedetto da Maiano (busts of Giotto and Squarcialupi), Andrea del Castagno (monument of Nicolò da Tolentino), Paolo Uccello (monument of Giovanni Acuto), Domenico di Michelino (portrait of Dante). The apse is dominated by Brunelleschi's dome, decorated with frescoes by Giorgio Vasari and Federico Zuccari (Last Judgement, 1579) and stained-glass windows made from cartoons by Donatello, Ghiberti, Paolo Uccello and Andrea del Castagno. In the

9

◀ *Cathedral façade.*

centre of the octagon there is the choir and the high altar (with a «Crucifix» by Benedetto da Maiano) the works of Baccio Bandinelli and Giovanni Bandini. Here is the entrance to the two Sacristies: the «Sacristia Vecchia» on the right, with a terracotta by Luca della Robbia in the lunette of the entrance and, inside, various paintings of XV-XVI century; the «Sacristia Nuova», in which Lorenzo the Magnificent took shelter during the Pazzi Plot (April 26, 1478) is on the left; it is closed by a bronze gate which has in the lunette above a terracotta, both of them the work of Luca della Robbia. In the central chapel of the apse there is a bronze sarcophagus, the reliquiary of S. Zanobi, a masterpiece by Ghiberti. Finally, in the first chapel of the left apse, there is the «Pietà», an impressive marble sculpture by Michelangelo belonging to the last period of the artist (1550-53).

GIOTTO'S BELL-TOWER

It is a splendid example of Gothic Florentine architecture for the elegance of its structure, the refined marble panelling and its plastic decoration. The bell-tower was begun in 1334 by Giotto and, after his death, the work was carried on by Andrea Pisano and later completed, in 1359, by Francesco Talenti. It is 84.70 metres high and stands on a base 14.45 metres high; from the terrace at the top, which can be reached by climbing 414 steps, the panorama embraces the whole town and the surrounding hills.

Its structure, supported by four corner pilasters, consists of a base divided into two sectors (the first one was built while Giotto was alive), then there are the two floors by Andrea Pisano and finally the three higher ones built by Talenti (of the latter the first two are perforated by two mullioned windows, the third one by a magnificent pointed three-mullioned window).

The base is decorated with a series of bas-reliefs which have now been substituted by copies (the originals being in the Museum of the Opera del Duomo). The cycle in the first sector, the «Creation and Life of Man», is by Andrea Pisano, Nanni di Bartolo and Luca della Robbia and, at least part of it, is from designs by Giotto. In the second sector there are the «Planets», the «Virtues», the «Liberal Arts» and the «Sacraments», executed by pupils of Andrea Pisano and, probably, of Alberto Arnoldi. Above the base one can see the niches which contained 16 statues of «Prophets», «Sybils» and of the «Baptist», the work of Donatello and other Florentine artists of XIV and XV century. Some of these statues have been replaced with copies; the originals are kept in the Museum of the Opera del Duomo.

10

MUSEUM OF THE OPERA DEL DUOMO

The museum houses many of the works of art from the Duomo, the Bell-tower and the Baptistry. Its main point of interest is the XIV and XV century Florentine sculpture. The hall of the old façade of the Duomo contains, among other works, some «Virgins», «Santa Reparata» and the «Statue of Boniface VIII» by Arnolfo di Cambio, «St. John» by Donatello and «St. Luke» by Nanni di Banco; in the adjoining rooms there are some architectural fragments, illuminated codices and jewellery. On the upper floor are housed the two famous «Cantorie» (choirs) by Luca della Robbia and Donatello which, in the past, were in the octagon of the dome in the Duomo. In the same room the 16 statues from the niches of the Bell-tower are on display, the work of Andrea Pisano, Nanni di Bartolo and Donatello (of the latter one should remember «Habbakuk» and «Abraham and Isaac»). In the following rooms there are the panels from the bell-tower, the work of Andrea Pisano, Luca della Robbia, Alberto Arnoldi and others; finally there is the well-known «altar of the Baptistry», an exceptional work of jewellers' art which took over 114 years to create. There are also some paintings of XIV century in this museum.

Donatello: The Choir.

Luca della Robbia: The Choir (detail).

The Baptistry.

THE BAPTISTRY

Consecrated to St. John the Baptist, patron saint of the city, the Baptistry was probably built in the XI century on a previous paleo-christian construction of which some remains have been found in the foundations. But, because of even older remains, it is believed that a pagan temple, probably dedicated to Mars, had previously occupied this area. The Baptistry is octagonal in shape and is framed by a double series of pilasters surmounted by an octagonal pyramid shaped roof, with sides corresponding to the ones of the octagon; its architecture is clearly Romanesque with decorations in coloured marble. It is to be noted that the apse was added in a subsequent period, probably towards 1202.

Until 1128 this building was used as the cathedral of the city, then it became what it is now; Dante Alighieri was baptized within its walls.

The most important elements of its structure are without any doubt the three doors, unmatched masterpieces of two great artists: Andrea Pisano for the oldest door and Lorenzo Ghiberti for the other two.

EAST DOOR (facing the Duomo): It is considered the masterpiece of Ghiberti (1378-1455) and executed, with the help of Michelozzo, Benozzo Gozzoli and Bernardo Cennini, between 1425 and 1452; Michelangelo named it «Porta del Paradiso» (Gate of Paradise). In the ten panels which form this door are represented «Scenes from the Old Testament» which show an extraordinary pictorial

and perspective relief, typical of the Renaissance. The precious ornamental framework is adorned with statuettes of «Prophets», and «Sybils» alternating with busts of contemporary artists, among whom is Lorenzo Ghiberti.

The difference in style between the North Door and the «Paradise» door is quite amazing; the artist was a young man when he began the former and an old man when he completed the latter. Fifty years of work; his workshop, where the rules of the new art were formed, became the centre for XV century research and experimentation; numerous artists came and went and significantly contributed to the setting up of this new art; Ghiberti himself was the focal point and summarized in his work the efforts of a whole period.

The two porphyry columns at the sides of the door were presented to Florence by Pisa, in 1117, as a token of gratitude for the help received during the war against the Saracens in the Balearic Islands.

Above the trabeation there is a marble group, «Jesus and the Baptist» (1502) by Andrea Sansovino and an «Angel» (1792) by Lorenzo Spinazzi.

NORTH DOOR: This is the first one of the two made by Ghiberti (1403-24), commissioned after the well-known competition which took place in 1401, in which even Brunelleschi among other artists took part (the two sketches are kept in the National Museum).

It is divided into 28 panels of which the 20 upper ones represent «Stories of the New Testament» and the remaining 8 the «Evangelists and the Doctors of the Church». Its elegant style can be ascribed to the late Gothic period.

Above the trabeation there is a bronze sculpture, «The Baptist between the Levite and the Pharisee» (1506-11) by Giovan Francesco Rustici.

SOUTH DOOR: This one is the oldest of the three doors and it was made by Andrea Pisano in 1330. Its design is Gothic; the 20 upper panels represent «Stories of the Baptist» and the 8 lower ones the «Cardinal and Theological Virtues».

The Renaissance decorative framework is adorned with foliage, birds and heads of angels, the work of Vittorio Ghiberti, Lorenzo's son.

The statues above the portal, «The Baptist between Salome and the Headsman» (1571) are by Vincenzo Danti.

THE INTERIOR: Its plan is octagonal with walls divided in three sections by monolithic columns, and covered with marble slabs, on which rests the high ogival radial dome. The architectural structure is Romanesque, but it still shows some medieval features. The apse and the dome are decorated with mosaics which are a precious example of XII century painting. The ones in the apse, the work of friar Jacopo (1225), represent, in a style with Byzantine influence, the «Agnello Mistico» with, on either side, the «Virgin with Child» and the «Baptist in Throne». The mosaics in the dome, made between the first half of the XIII century and 1330, by Venetian artists, on cartoons by Florentine artists (among them Cimabue) in-

Ghiberti's Door, east side, defined by Michelangelo as the «Door of Paradise». ▶

12

Baptistry interior: Byzantine mosaics of the cupola or dome dating to the 14th century.

clude «Stories of Genesis» with the «Creatio of the World» and the «Flood», «Stories of th Baptist, of Christ and Joseph». On the portio of the dome corresponding to the apse ther is the great figure of «Christ», now ascribed t Coppo di Marcovaldo, and the «Last Judg ment» with the terrifying representation «Hell». The font is of Pisan school (1371); th inlaid floor with the signs of the zodiac an oriental ornaments dates back, it is thoug to 1209.

Along the walls these should be noted: o the right of the apse the «Tomb of the ant pope Giovanni XXIII», the work of Donatel with the help of Michelozzo; on the left, be tween two Roman sarcophagi, the splend and tragic «Magdalene», wood sculpture, th too by Donatello and ascribed to the perio 1435-55.

East Door: Panel depicting the finding of the silve cup in Benjamin's sack.

Via Calzaioli: Left, Church of Orsanmichele's façade and, right, the Palazzo dell'Arte della Lana.

Orsanmichele Church: Interior.

CHURCH OF ORSANMICHELE

Its name comes from the earlier church of San Michele in Orto (St Michael in the Garden) which was demolished in 1284 to make way for a grain-market loggia. The present church of Orsanmichele was built between 1337 and 1404 by, in order of succession, the architects Francesco Talenti, Neri di Fioravante, Benci di Cione and Simone Talenti.

The ground floor was originally an open loggia. The exterior arcade was sealed in 1380 and raised to two storeys with double-light mullion windows. The building itself is an outstanding example of Florentine Gothic as typified by the ornate style of the ground floor's trefoil arches and the pillars' tabernacles (canopied recesses) designed to house the statues of the Patron Saints of the Arts.

The interior, with its two pillared aisles and traces of 14-th century frescoes, features superb stained glass windows. At the end of the righthand aisle is the famous 1340 tabernacle by Andrea Orcagna, with its intarsia of stones, glass chips and mortar inlay, one of the Florentine Gothic's most beautiful works. In the same via or street is the **PALAZZO DELL'ARTE DELLA LANA** (The Wool Guild Hall). Built in the Trecento (14th century), it is today the home of the Dante Society. The structure comprises a tower house and a smaller building. By passing through its interior, one gains entrance to the two magnificent upper rooms of Orsanmichele.

Piazza della Signoria.

Neptune's Fountain.

PIAZZA DELLA SIGNORIA

This vast piazza, which today, with its monuments and works of art, constitutes the most fascinating place in the city, has been the scene of many of the most significant events of the city's history from the Middle Ages up to the present time. Even today various large public ceremonies take place here: the Flowers Show of the Maggio Fiorentino, the Florentine May Festival, and the traditional and famous «Gioco del calcio», Game of Football in 16th century costume. Here we can admire the magnificent and imposing Palazzo della Signoria (Palazzo Vecchio). The original construction, of 1298-1314, is traditionally attributed to Arnolfo di Cambio, and it was extended by Buontalenti and Vasari. The old nucleus on an irregular plan is in rusticated ashlar, with two floors with elegant mullions and a crenellated balcony and Torre di Arnolfo, giving a sense of powerful mass. On the left of the palazzo, the grandiose Neptune fountain (Biancone). It was ordered by Cosimo I from Bartolomeo Ammannati. The bronze statues which decorated the fountain are the work of Ammannati himself and other collaborators, including Giambologna. A porphyry disc, in front of the fountain, marks the spot on which Girolamo Savonarola and his companions were burnt at the stake on the 23rd May, 1498. On the left of the fountain an equestrian monument of the Grand-Duke Cosimo I dei Medici, by Giambologna; the bas-reliefs on the base show three important episodes from the life of Cosimo I. At the end of

16

the piazza the 14th century Palazzo Mercanzia, with, on its façade, the crest of the Florentine Guilds. On the left the Palazzo Ugaccioni to a design by Mariotto di Zanobi.

LOGGIA OF THE SEIGNORY OR CITY HALL

Also known as the Loggia dell'Orcagna, to whom it is attributed by tradition, and the Loggia dei Lanzi, as the Lansquenet mercenaries were garrisoned here, it was actually designed by Benci di Cione and Simone Talenti and built from 1376-81. Late Florentine Gothic in style, the Signoria was the seat of such official city ceremonies as the election and proclamation of the Gonfalonier (standard bearer) and the city Priors (magistrates).

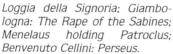
Loggia della Signoria; Giambologna: The Rape of the Sabines; Menelaus holding Patroclus; Benvenuto Cellini: Perseus.

Portrait of Leonardo da Vinci.

Panorama of Florence. ▶

18

Portrait of Galileo Galilei.

PALAZZO DELLA SIGNORIA

Until the 16th century the palace was the seat of the Governors, subsequently the home of Cosimo I dei Medici; from 1865-1871 the House of Deputies of the Kingdom of Italy had its first sittings here; it was also the home of the Ministry of Foreign Affairs; since 1872 it has been the seat of the Municipio.

INTERIOR: We enter the courtyard, restored and renovated by Michelozzo in 1453, richly decorated with stuccos and pictures depicting the marriage of Francesco dei Medici to Giovanna of Austria. In the middle a fountain with the bowl in porphyry and above it a beautiful bronze «Dolphin and Putto» by Andrea del Verrocchio (the original is preserved inside). In the niche above the door «Sampson and a Philistine» by Pierino da Vinci; on the left side of the courtyard the Arms Room, one of the few remaining parts of the 13th century building. Between this courtyard and the second, which has pillars by Cronaca, the Vasari staircase taking us to the upper floors and the Monumental Apartments.

First Floor. Among the many important rooms located here, the magnificent Salone dei Cinquecento (Hall of the Five Hundred) is by far the most imposing in grandeur. The work of Cronaca (1495), it was designed as the seat of the Consiglio Maggiore (the city's Council of Elders) and embellished by the works of Vasari and his school. Also by Vasari are the Studio of Francesco I (1570-72) and the Tesoretto (private or secret scriptorium) of Cosimo I. There follow in order the Sala (room) of the Otto di Pratica (Eight of Practice) with its fine wooden ceiling by Benedetto da Maiano and Marco del Tasso, Sala dei Dugento (Room of the Two Hundred) stately furbished by the lacunar or coffered ceiling with Benedetto da Maiano's fleur-de-lys intaglio, the Quartiere di Leone X (quarters of Pope Leo X) ornately rendered by the artistry of Vasari and his pupils, the Cappella (chapel) of Leo X in which are found Raphael's Madonna dell'Impannata and Vasari's Sts Cosma and Damian, and, finally, the Sala of Pope Clement VII with its fresco of Florence under seige (1529).

Second Floor. The first room we come to is the Quartiere degli Elementi (Quarters of the Elements) by Bernardo del Tasso (1550) and frescoed by Vasari and Cristoforo Gherardi.

Palazzo della Signoria: Michelozzo's courtyard and the Salone dei Cinquecento.

Palazzo del Bargello.

THE NATIONAL MUSEUM OF THE «BARGELLO»

The construction of this severe building which is, in order of importance, the second best civil building of the medieval city after the Palazzo della Signoria, was begun

Luca della Robbia: Madonna del Roseto.

Donatello: David.

in 1255, probably by two Dominican architects: fra' Sisto and fra' Ristoro. Built to be the seat of the «Captain of the People», in 1261 it became the seat of the Podestà, from 1502 it housed the Council of Justice and subsequently, from 1574, the Captain of Justice or Bargello (hence the name of the building).

After a long period in which the Bargello was also used as a prison, with the restoration begun in 1857 the building was returned to its original architectural shape and freed from the superstructures which had altered its aspect.

Since 1859 it has been a museum, and certainly one of the most important in the world for the appreciation of Tuscan sculpture from XIV to XVII century (mainly for the works by Donatello, the Della Robbia, and Michelangelo) but also for the other collections it houses (arms, bronzes, porcelains, medals, goldsmith's works and fabrics).

26

THE UFFIZI GALLERY

The building which houses one of the world's most famous art galleries (certainly the most important in Italy) and the «Archivio di Stato» (Record Office) was begun in 1560 by Vasari in late-Renaissance style, and completed in 1580 by Alfonso Parigi and Bernardo Buontalenti according to Vasari's project. This enormous building, devised by order of Cosimo I to contain the administrative offices and the archives of the Florentine State, flanks the long square with a portico interrupted by a wide arch with a view of the Arno. After every second column of the portico there is a pilaster with a niche containing a statue of outstanding Tuscan personalities, from Dante to Petrarca, from Leonardo to Michelangelo, from Cosimo to Lorenzo il Magnifico. The gallery offers an unparalleled and complete collection of Florentine and Tuscan painting, and also contains many works of other Italian schools (the most represented is the Venetian one), a group of Flemish paintings, extremely important because of the influence they had on Italian painting, the famous collection of self-portraits and a great number of ancient sculptures (some of them of great importance like the «Venus of the Medici» of the I century B.C., derived from Prassiteles, or the «Knife-Grinder», the «Wrestlers» and «Dionysus and the Satyr»).

Palazzo degli Uffizi and Palazzo Vecchio.

Crucifix depicting the Passion (Tuscan school of the 12th century).

Piero della Francesca: Battista Sforza and Federico da Montefeltre.
Giorgio Vasari: Lorenzo il Magnifico. *Filippo Lippi: Self-portrait.*

Left, Fra' Filippo Lippi: Madonna and Child with angels. Above, Sandro Botticelli: The Allegory of Spring. Centre, Leonardo da Vinci: The Annunciation. Right, detail of the Annunciation.

29

Sandro Botticelli: The Birth of Venus.

chelangelo: The Holy Family.

Sandro Botticelli: Madonna and Child of the Magnificat.

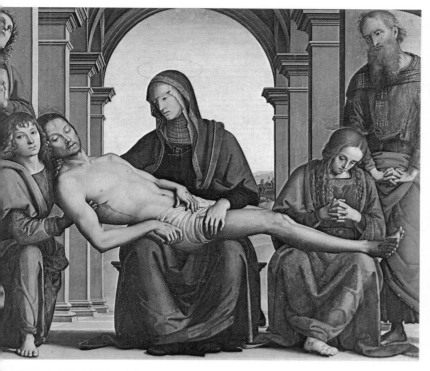

Above, Perugino: The Pietà. Right, R. Sanzio: The Madonna del Cardellino.
Titian: Venus with Dog. Caravaggio: The Sacrifice of Isaac. Right, Titian: Flora.

PONTE VECCHIO

So called because it is the oldest bridge in the city, it is said that it was first built by the Etruscans and later rebuilt by the Romans, but this is uncertain. It is known, however, that from 1080 there was a wooden bridge here which was rebuilt in stone in 1177 and later destroyed in the terrible flood of 1333. In 1345 it was re-

Panoramic views of the Arno and Ponte Vecchio.

constructed with three solid arches, probably by Neri di Fioravante, and the characteristic rows of shops along its side date back to that period. They were at first used by butchers, but in the second half of the XVI century they were assigned to gold and silversmiths, whose work may still be admired today.

33

BASILICA OF SAN LORENZO

The church of S. Lorenzo is situated in the square of the same name where there is also a picturesque market.

This church is a very ancient one and was built on the site of another one, consecrated in 393 by St. Ambrogio, Bishop of Milan.

It was built, the first time, in pre-Romanesque style (c. 1000 A.D.) and rebuilt, from 1421, in its present form by Filippo Brunelleschi to the order of Giovanni di Bicci de' Medici.

The interior has three aisles separated by Corinthian columns. The two pulpits underneath the last two spans of the central nave are by Donatello.

At the foot of the high altar three bronze gratings mark the place in which Cosimo the Elder, called «Pater Patriae», was buried. The Old Sacristy, conceived by Brunelleschi, houses important works by Donatello and Andrea Cavalcanti; underneath the archway, on the left, is a bronze and porphyry sarcophagus by Verrocchio.

San Lorenzo Basilica: Interior and Cloisters.

THE MEDICI CHAPELS

At the back of S. Lorenzo are found the «Cappella dei Principi» and the «Sagrestia Nuova», the first one connected with the apse and the second one connected with the right transept.

Through a large crypt, designed by Buontalenti, where some members of the Medici family are buried, one ascends to the «Cappella dei Principi»; this chapel is considered a significant example of Baroque architecture, though it is apparent that the richness of the decoration and the materials used were aimed at inspiring a sense of wonder. It was begun in 1604 by Nigetti on a design by Giovanni de' Medici (subsequently altered by Buontalenti); it is octagonal in shape, and surmounted by a dome; its construction took until late in the XVIII century.

In the chapel there are six enormous sarcophagi dedicated to the grand dukes buried in the vault beneath. On the second and third sarcophagus there are two big gilded bronze statues, the work of Ferdinando Tacca (XVII cent.).

Through a corridor one enters the «Sagrestia Nuova» which, though somewhat similar in shape to the chapel by Brunelleschi, very clearly shows the novelty of Michelangelo's genius in the dramatic tension of the architectural structures and decorative elements.

Medici Chapels.

This mausoleum of the Medici family was begun by Michelangelo who worked at it from 1521 to 1533 (a little later he transferred to Rome) and completed in 1555 by Vasari and Ammannati.

It was to contain four sepulchral monuments, but those of Lorenzo the Magnificent and his brother Giuliano were not made because Michelangelo left Florence. The two the artist left are among the most beautiful works of Buonarroti.

Quite a number of hypotheses have been made to interpret the allegorical significance of the chapel, all of them too elaborate and too literary to be worth mentioning here, not least because they cannot be verified due to the fact that this monument is so incomplete. It is interesting, though, to mention Jacob Burckhardt's opinion: «Architecture and sculpture are here conceived in such a closely linked way that it seems as if the artist has moulded them out of the very same clay».

Though contested by other art critics, this judgement is still basically valid and stresses the impression that most of the visitors get.

On the left is the «Sepulchre of Lorenzo», duke of Urbino, grandson to Lorenzo the Magnificent, with the statue of the duke (called «Il Pensieroso» — pensive — as he seems lost in deep thought) and the recumbent statues of «Dawn» and «Dusk».

Burial Chapel of the Medici Princes.

The Sacrestia Nuova (Michelangelo).

35

Cupola's Ceiling.

Tomb of Lorenzo de' Medici.

On the right is the «Sepulchre of Giuliano», duke of Nemours, the third son of Lorenzo the Magnificent, with the idealized statue of the duke represented as a young warrior, and the statues of «Day» and «Night».

These four allegoric statues, symbolising the relentless passing of time, certainly count among the most important achievements in sculptre of all time.

It is interesting to note how the artist used marbles of different colours («Night» is almost white, «Day» is almost dark, etc.), thus adding a characteristic chromatic feature to the tension of the plastic forms.

Leaning against the wall facing the altar there is a big plain marble case containing the bodies of Lorenzo the Magnificent and his brother Giuliano. Above it three statues have been placed (probably at Vasari's wish): a «Virgin with Child», also by Michelangelo and, at its sides, «St. Cosmas» by Montorsoli and «St. Damian» by Raffaello da Montelupo.

«Michelangelo», Goldscheider wrote, «did not try to make true portraits of the two Dukes in these statues: to the Florentines who were puzzled because of this purely idealistic conception, lacking any similarity, Michelangelo proudly answered that in a thousand years' time nobody would know what the real features of the Medici were like. Lorenzo represents contemplative life, Giuliano active life, as it has already been suggested by Jonathan Richardson».

It is worth mentioning here three opinions Goldscheider himself quoted. The one by Stendhal: «The statues of S. Lorenzo are partially unfinished. This, however, is an advantage, because of Michelangelo's powerful style». The one by Burckhardt: «In these four statues the "Maestro" has expressed his most daring ideas on the limitations and aims of his art... while, for his successors, this was the quickest way to failure». And, finally, Vasari's: «What could I say about "Night", not a rare statue, but a unique one? Who has ever seen, in any century and in any art, old or modern, statues created in this way, expressing not only the quietness of sleep but also the grief and melancholy for the loss of something great and honoured? One has to believe that this is "that" night which, for a long period, would overshadow all those artists, both in sculpture and design, who thought it possible not to surpass him but only to equal him».

THE CHURCH OF S. MARIA NOVELLA

It stands on the North side of a wide pentagonal square where two obelisks, the work of Giambologna, used to mark the route of the old «Palio dei Cocchi» (chariot races), and faces the XV century «Loggia di S. Paolo» built after Brunelleschi's Portico degli Innocenti.

This outstanding masterpiece of Gothic architecture was begun by two Dominican friars, Sisto and Ristoro, in 1246 (the aisles in 1279) and completed, in 1360, by Jacopo Talenti.

The splendid façade, begun in 1300, was continued between 1456 and 1470 by Leon Battista Alberti, who also made the top section and the portal.

The interior, Latin cross shaped, is divided into three aisles by polystyle pillars supporting wide arches and pointed vaults where the Gothic impetus is mitigated by a typically Latin sense of spaciousness.

Among the many works of art housed in this church, worthy of special mention are the frescoes by Filippino Lippi in the Strozzi Chapel, those of Domenico Ghirlandaio in the Major Chapel, the «Crucifix» by Brunelleschi (the only sculpture on wood he left) in the Gondi Chapel, an exceptional and very human «Crucifix» on wood by Giotto in the Sacristy and the famous fresco by Masaccio, the «Holy Trinity, the Virgin Mary and St. John» on the third arch of the left aisle.

Santa Maria Novella: Interior.

Santa Maria Novella Church. ▶

Santa Maria Novella: Masaccio: The Blessed Trinity.

Benozzo Gozzoli: Fresco (detail).

PALAZZO MEDICI RICCARDI

(On the corner of via Martelli and via Cavour). This fine Renaissance palace was constructed by Michelozzo in 1440-1460, for Cosimo il Vecchio dei Medici (Pater Patriae). Among the successors of Cosimo who lived here were: Catherine dei Medici, Queen of France; the Emperor Charles V; Charles VIII, the King of France and the Duke Alessandro Medici. The building is on three floors in ashlar, of imposing elegance with its rich friezes and fine centred mullions. We enter the courtyard by the portico. Above the arches is a decoration of medallions attributed to Bertoldo, a pupil of Donatello's. The designs are by Maso di Bartolomeo, 1452. The first floor is mullioned and the loggia is in ionic style. From the courtyard, on the left we come to the Museo Mediceo, given over to periodic exhibitions showing the glory of the Medicis. In the first room «Madonna and Child» by Filippo Lippi, one of the artist's best works. Return to the courtyard and through the first door on the right we go up to the Cappella Medici. This contains a large fresco by Benozzo Gozzoli (1459) which shows the Wise Men on the way to Bethlehem. In this various members of the Medici are vividly shown; also the Patriarch of Costantinople and the Eastern Emperor John VII Paleologue. On the right wall on the left corner we see the self-portrait of the artist. Return to the courtyard and by the door under the portico we can come to the gallery constructed for Riccardi, and frescoed by Luca Giordano in 1683 with the «Apotheosis of the Medici».

Benozzo Gozzoli: Procession of the Magi (detail).

38

THE CHURCH AND MONASTERY OF SAN MARCO

They were built in 1299 by the Silvestrine monks on a preexisting oratory, then rebuilt and enlarged by Michelozzo (1437-52) at Cosimo the Elder's wish and made over to the Dominicans of Fiesole. While the church has been extensively altered, through the centuries, the Monastery (in which, among others, the Beato Angelico lived, and also S. Antonino, Savonarola and Fra Bartolomeo, a very remarkable painter of the early XVI century) still retains the harmonious lines of its Renaissance structure. Since 1869 it has housed the «Museo dell'Angelico»; Angelico, in fact, for many years worked there, leaving about one hundred works, also including those from other places.

Fra Giovanni da Fiesole, known as the Beato Angelico (1400-1455), was one of the outstanding painters of the XV century; his style for a long period was wrongly considered in striking contrast to Masaccio's though he soon learned Masaccio's perspective and humanistic lesson; it is true, though, that the spirituality permeating his works is almost transcendent, quite the opposite to Masaccio's intensely human conception but, however, his culture was extremely modern; for this reason the intensity and the mystical atmosphere of his style and form should not be considered as being of a Gothic tradition and this can be proved by the interest and the attention Piero della Francesca paid to Angelico's spacial conception. Among the most impressive and interesting works of this artist, the «Flight into Egypt», the «Last Judgement», the «Crucifixion» and the stupendous «Annunciation», are the ones which best convey the authentic meaning of Angelico.

Piazza and Church of San Marco.

Ghirlandaio: The Last Supper.

Beato Angelico: Annunciation.

GALLERIA DELL'ACCADEMIA

The entrance to the gallery is in Via Ricasoli along the arcades of the Academy of Fine Arts.

The wide and solemn lobby is decorated with Flemish Tapestries of the XVI Century, all of them showing stories of Genesis. In the Gallery there are sculptures by Michelangelo and paintings of the Tuscan school.

In the first room are the four statues of the «Captives» made by Michelangelo for the tomb of Pope Julius II in Rome.

Towards the end of the room, on the right, is the «Pietà Palestrina» from the chapel in the Church of Palestrina.

Below the dome of the Gallery, is the splendid masterpiece of Michelangelo's juvenile period, «David».

This statue, begun in 1501 was finished three years later. Formerly placed at the entrance of Palazzo Vecchio, it was subsequently moved to the Academy Gallery.

Michelangelo: David ▶

Michelangelo's David (detail).

The Tribuna: Michelangelo: David.

BASILICA OF SANTA CROCE

It faces the square of Santa Croce which, on the other sides, is lined by old palaces.

In this square, during the Medici period, first the tournaments and later foot-ball matches took place.

The church belongs to the Franciscans and was built towards 1295, according to plans by Arnolfo di Cambio.

The façade is a modern one (1863) and so is the bell-tower (1865) built in gothic style.

The interior, in the shape of an Egyptian cross is divided into three aisles by octagonal pillars supporting pointed arches.

The main nave has an open-beam roof while the choir and the chapels in the transept have vaulted roofs.

Santa Croce Basilica

Santa Croce: Annunciation (Donatello).

Santa Croce: Interior.

Palazzo Pitti.

THE PITTI PALACE

Sandro Botticelli: Portrait of a Young Man.

It was begun after 1457 by Luca Fancelli on a project that Filippo Brunelleschi had made in 1440 for Luca Pitti, a rich merchant who was a friend and later a rival of the Medici; this imposing palace, with boldly rusticated masonry, stands on the slope of the Boboli hill and was conceived with rigid geometrical proportions which were fortunately respected in the subsequent additions.

It consists of a ground floor with three doors alternating with four rectangular windows, and two upper-floors, each of them with a balcony connecting seven French windows; after a period during which work was interrupted and the palace sold to the Medici, from 1558 it was enlarged, first by Ammannati who inserted two windows where the side doors had been and built the inner courtyard. Later on Giulio Parigi (1620) added three windows to each side, and his son Alfonso (1640), with additions to the ground-floor and the first floor, brought the façade to its present aspect.

Finally, the two wings, called «rondò», were added during the second half of the XVIII century on a project by Giuseppe Ruggieri. The main door leads into the Ammannati courtyard, flanked on three sides by the inner façade and the wings and on the fourth side by the terrace which looks onto the Boboli gardens (in the central arcade is the XVII century «Grotto of Moses» and, at ground level, the «Fountain of the Artichoke», the work of Francesco del Tadda and Francesco Susini).

The palace was first the residence of the Medici and later of the Lorraine; then, in 1860, it went to the Savoy royal family who lived there during the years when Florence was the capital of Italy (1865-71).

At present it houses the Palatina Gallery, the «Gallery of Modern Art», the «Silver Museum» and the «Museum of Carriages». It is also possible to visit the «old royal apartments».

◀ *Raffaello Sanzio: The Madonna of the Grand Duke.*   *The Iliad Room.*

Guido Reni: The Child Bacchus.   *Raffaello Sanzio: Madonna della Seggiola.*

THE BOBOLI GARDENS

These gardens, one of the most beautiful and typical examples of an Italian style garden, lie on the Boboli hill between the Pitti Palace, the fortress of Belvedere and Porta Romana.

The gardens were commissioned by Eleonora da Toledo, and work was begun in 1550 on a design by Tribolo, then continued by Ammannati and Buontalenti and completed in the XVII century by other artists. They are full of delightful spots with splendid trees and flowers; everything — setting, landscape, fountains and statues — contributes to their enchanting atmosphere.

Immediately beyond the entrance there is the «Fountain of little Bacchus», with the statue of Pietro Barbino, Cosimo I's dwarf, riding a tortoise; mention must now be made of the «Grotto of Buontalenti» (1583-88), decorated with paintings by Poccetti, and with several sculptures, including «Venus coming out of the water» by Giambologna (1573); the XVII century «Anfiteatro» with a big granite basin and several statues; the «Vivaio di Nettuno», a large basin with a rock in the middle surmounted by the «statue of Neptune», the work of Stoldo Lorenzi; and, finally, the «Piazzale dell'Isolotto» where, on the little island in the middle of the pretty lake, there is the splendid «Fountain of the Ocean» by Giambologna.

Boboli Gardens: Neptune's Fountain.

Boboli Gardens: Ocean's Fountain.

Boboli Gardens: Ocean's Fountain.

THE PIAZZALE MICHELANGELO

Built in 1868 by the architect Giuseppe Poggi, this large square has as its focal point the monument to Michelangelo, which includes some copies of his most famous works, above which stands his David, looking down onto the city below.

From this fascinating spot, a traditional walk both for Florentines and foreigners, one can admire the city from above but, being at the same time so close, it is possible to single out each individual monument, appreciating architectural and artistic values. The city nestles in the green hills and spreads along the banks of the Arno, with a series of bridges and the Ponte Vecchio in the foreground.

Behind the square, high among the cypresses, stands the beautiful church of «S. Salvatore al Monte» built in 1475 by Cronaca.

FORT OF BELVEDERE

Erected by Bernardo Buontalenti in 1590-95, on orders from Ferdinando I dei Medici, to protect the palazzo Pitti below and to improve the city's defences on that side. It is composed of a central palazzetto, surrounded by a large glacis, from which we enjoy various views of the city and the surrounding countryside. Nowadays the buildings are used for important exhibitions.

Continuing along viale Galileo we come to the piazzale of the same name, from which viale Machiavelli, still flanked by gardens and greenery, leads us to Porta Romana.

THE CHURCH OF S. MINIATO AL MONTE

S. Miniato stands at the top of the «Monte alle Croci» hill where one can enjoy the splendid panorama of the city and its surrounding area.

It was built after 1018 by order of Bishop Ildebrando over an earlier building and was completed at the beginning of 1200. Together with the Baptistry of St. John, it is the most important example of Florentine Romanesque architecture.

The façade, completed in the XIII century, is decorated with a geometrical pattern of white and green marble slabs. Its lower section is partitioned by five blind arches on which three doors open alternately, while the upper section, corresponding to the nave only, is divided into three parts by means of slender pilaster strips; above the central window, shaped in almost classic style, there is a XIII century mosaic on a gilded background («Christ enthroned between the Virgin and S. Miniato»).

The pediment, sloping on both sides, is decorated with sham arches. The interior, which has kept almost untouched its XI century lay-out, is divided into three aisles by polystyle columns and pilasters with the presbytery raised above the crypt beneath.

The latter is divided into three naves and closed by a 1207 marble screen, on which the splendid «pulpit» rests. On the Romanesque altar there is a «Crucifix», ascribed to Luca della Robbia.

San Miniato al Monte Basilica.

San Miniato al Monte Basilica: Interior.

FIESOLE

This ancient town of Etruscan origin became fairly important in the Roman Age, particularly during the imperial period. After the Barbarian invasions it even ruled over Florence, which in 1125 succeeded in conquering it, thus determinating its political decay.

The very heart of the town is the Mino da Fiesole square where, in ancient times, the Roman Forum was.

Here one can admire the «Cathedral», and, further above, the XIV century «Palazzo Pretorio» together with the «Oratory of S. Maria Primerana».

The XI cent. Romanesque «Cathedral» was extensively restored and enlarged in the following centuries. The interior consists of three aisles with a raised presbytery; on the altar there is a beautiful «polyptych» by Bicci di Lorenzo. Very interesting is the «Salutati Chapel» with frescoes by Cosimo Rosselli and the «tomb of Bishop Leonardo Salutati», the work of Mino da Fiesole (1464).

THE ROMAN THEATRE: A street at the back of the Cathedral leads to the «Roman Theatre» which is included in the archaeological area; here too is the «Museum» which houses architectural fragments, together with marble and fictile fragments of sculptures of the Etruscan, Roman and Barbarian periods, found during the excavations of the Theatre and in the archaeological area nearby.

The «Theatre», probably built before the I cent. A.D., was adorned and enlarged in the following centuries to hold up to 3,000 people and it still retains its cavea with three rows of seats and 19 steps.

To the right of the Theatre one can see the ruins of the «Thermae» and, further ahead, the «Etruscan-Roman Temple» of which only the steps and the base of a few columns remain. To the right of the Temple are the ruins of a Gate together with a long section of the Etruscan walls.

From the Mino da Fiesole square one climbs up to the «Church of S. Francesco» which stands on the hill where the ancient «Acropolis» was. From the terrace a splendid view of Florence can be enjoyed. The church, Gothic in style and consisting of a single aisle, contains some works of art of important artistic value. Adjoining the church there is the charming «Little cloister of S. Bernardino».

49

Fiesole: Panorama.

Fiesole: Church of San Francesco

Fiesole: Roman Amphitheatre.

CERTALDO

Located in the beautiful Val d'Elsa, it is an important farm and industrial community. The town itself is divided into a modern district set on a rise called the Borgo and the walled medieval core atop a hill called the Castello.

Certaldo is noted as the birthplace of Giovanni Boccaccio (1313-1373), whose house in the Via of the same name can still be seen with its tower and loggia (today it is the seat of the Centro Nazionale di Studi sul Boccaccio, the National Centre for Boccaccio Studies). Above left: Town panorama. Above: Portrait of the writer. Adjacent: Palazzo Pretorio or Palazzo del Vicariato, home of the Counts of Alberti up to the 13th century and then of the Podestàs and Florentine Vicari.

VINCI

Part of Tuscany's renown is as the birthplace of numerous geniuses in literature, the arts and sciences. Leonardo (portrait on page 19) was born in Vinci on April 15th 1452. Painter, sculptor, architect, scientist and writer, genius in every sense of the term Renaissance man, he was endowed with one of the brightest intellects ever to have cast its light on the stage of history and to have raised the aspirations of man to a spiritual universality.

As with many of the great figures of the Italian Renaissance, Leonardo the man is to be found at the core of his art, surrounded as it were by the landscape most congenial to him. He represents man totally unfettered of the bonds of any religious dogma. Even when it comes to depicting a saint, as with the 1481 St Jerome in the Vatican Gallery, Leonardo's art portrays him without any hint of mysticism.

Vinci originally developed round the 12th-century Castello dei Conti Guidi at the foothills of Monte Albano. Historically, the town was placed under Florentine rule from 1263. The Castello or fortress (see photo above), once the seat of the tribunal, was restored in 1940 and today houses the Museo Vinciniano.

Right: The house in which Leonardo was born. The town celebrates his birth every year on April 15th with a series of cultural events.

CERRETO GUIDI

Situated atop a faintly discernible knoll, this charming and picturesque town (right) is set amidst hillsides the beauty of which is matched only by the bounty of the gardens, vineyards and olive groves embroidering them, passim. The medieval fief of the Counts of Guidi as its name bears witness, Cerreto is famous for its Villa Medicea (bottom right), with its museum collection of art, and the parish church of San Leonardo housing works by Giovanni della Robbia, Giambologna, the school of Filippo Lippi and Cigoli. A circular square near the church offers a charming panorama of San Miniato, Monte Pisano, the Apuan Alps, Montecatini and Pistoia's Apennines.

51

VALLOMBROSA

Set on one of the peaks of Pratomagno along the provincial road at kilometre stone 225 on the western slope of Monte Secchieta is Vallombrosa. Founded next to the medieval monastery of Vallombrosani, it is a quiet village with facilities for winter skiing and summer holidays. Above: Scenic panorama and monastery, a castle-like building of the late 15th century with a bell tower dating to 1200 and a 15th-century tower.

VICCHIO

A friendly village atop a knoll encircled by a lush and verdant countryside, it is the birthplace of two great artists — Giotto (1267-1337) and Beato Angelico (b. late 14th-early 15th century). Its fortified walls, partly preserved today, were erected by the Florentines in 1324 and enabled the town's defenders to put up a heroic resistance in 1529-30 during the siege of the Republic of Florence by the imperial troops. The medieval core is represented by Piazza Giotto (below right) in which stand the Palazzo Pretorio and the Pieve di Santo Stefano. Left: Giotto's house.

PRATO

The archaeological evidence gathered to date would indicate an Etruscan-Roman settlement on the site of the present city. However that may be, what is certain is that, in the 9th century A.D., Prato began to expand growing out from the Pieve di Santo Stefano (the Duomo today). Situated mid-way in the flood plain stretching from Florence to Pistoia against the foothills of the Monti della Calvana, it was once ruled by the powerful Alberti family whose holdings covered an area from the Bolognese Apennines to the Valdinievole and from the Valdelsa to the Maremma. Today this city at the mouth of the Bisenzio river is an important centre of the textile industry and houses within its fortified hexagonal walls of the 14th century a formidable heritage of art and architecture tracing its history down through the centuries.

Right: Panorama, the Duomo and Piazza del Duomo. Below, from left to right: the church of Santa Maria delle Carceri, the Castello dell'Imperatore (Emperor's Castle) and Bacchus fountain.

PISTOIA

Known to the Romans as «Pistoria», the city dates perhaps as far back as the 2nd century A.D., according to the various objects and memorial stone tablets which have come to light over the years. There is an even earlier mention if we consider the passage in Sallust citing Catalina's rout in 62 A.D. An important farming, industrial and trade centre, Pistoia is circumscribed by the Ombrone lowlands to the east, the Arno river to the south, Monte Albano to the west and the Apennine foothills to the north. Despite the inroads of modern architecture in the planning and design of the city's new district, it still preserves its medieval heritage in the many buildings, sculptures and Pisan Gothic churches for which it is renowned.

Palazzo del Comune (left). Built by the Guelphs in 1294 as the city hall, this imposing sandstone building was the seat of the powerful lords who ruled the city for centuries. The façade rests on minimally pointed arches and features two-light mullion windows at the first storey and elegant three-light mullions ornately wrought with the blazons of the Medicis and pope Clement VII at the second.

Palazzo Pretorio or Courthouse (left). Literally the pretorian palace, it was built in 1367 and is notable for the double order of two-light mullion windows and decorative blazons punctuating the upper part.

54

Battistero (above). Gothic in style and rectangular in floor plan, the Baptistry was begun in 1338 by the architect Cellino di Nese, after the design by Andrea Pisano, and completed in 1359. The Duomo (above right). The original edifice dating to the 5th century A.D. was renovated in Pisan Romanesque during the 12th and 13th centuries. It boasts a formidable façade with three orders of loggias, an imposing bell tower and an interior renowned for its 14th- and 15th-century art works.

Ospedale del Ceppo (adjacent). Founded in the 13th or 14th century, the hospital was embellished by the addition of the front Florentine portico in 1514 and, later, of the enameled terra cotta frieze in the manner of the della Robbia school. Below: «To Bury the Dead», detail of the frieze.

MONTECATINI TERME

Situated along the Pistoia-to-Lucca road in a level stretch of the resplendent and verdant Val di Nievole lying at the foot of Montecatini, it is sheltered against chilling winds by its proximity to the Apennine foothills. The natural hot springs with which nature has endowed Montecatini have made the spa the «capital city of waters», one of the most famous thermal baths in all Europe.

A modern and dynamic town, Montecatini has been known since antiquity for its health-giving springs. Their value as a spa was recognised as early as the 14th-16th centuries, when they began to be frequented in earnest, but it was not until the years 1765-90 that they were systematically exploited, when the initial land reclamation works and the installation of the first facilities — the Terme Leopoldine Tettuccio — were undertaken. Updated through constant development since then, Montecatini's spa today offers a unique combination of tradition and innovation.

Its extensive lawns and gardens, modern spa facilities, sports grounds and leisure activities, well-appointed shops, elegant cafés, restaurants and night spots, and its extensive calendar of cultural and social events make Montecatini one of the most sought-after resorts in which to enjoy a truly relaxing and carefree holiday.

Photos: Town panorama, Tettuccio Baths (interior and grounds) and night view of City Centre.

ABETONE

It is without doubt the oldest, most well known and popular resort of the Apennine mountains. Its tourist fortunes are a direct measure of the amenities of its natural surroundings. At 1388 metres above sea level, Abetone sits atop these scenic peaks in the centre of 3700 hectares of magnificent forest land straddling the slopes between the Tuscany and Emilia-Romagna regions. Add to such scenic beauty the well-appointed hotels, modern ski facilities, winter sporting events calendar and summer excursion itineraries, and you have one of the most ideal resort areas with year-round activities to be found anywhere.

The name Abetone, literally big fir, derives from a giant fir tree which had to be felled during construction of the road linking Tuscany and the Emilia-Romagna in the late 1800s.

COLLODI

Famous the world over as the birthplace and childhood home of Carlo Lorenzini, author of **Pinocchio** under the pseudonym of Carlo Collodi, the town is quite picturesque in its own right. Divided into two parts, it boasts the beautiful and extensive gardens of Villa Garzoni below and the castle town with its special scenic amenities above. It has also become, of course, a major tourist attraction thanks to the little wooden boy, with people being drawn from everywhere to visit its imaginative Parco di Pinocchio (Pinocchio's Park).

Aerial view of Lucca with the Church of San Martino.

Glimpse of Lucca's beautiful monuments in the old city.

LUCCA

The aerial view of Lucca calls to mind a past that is more often forgotten than remote. Situated in an extensive flood plain bounded by the Apuan Alps and Monte Pisano, to the left of the Serchio river, and completely encircled by its 16th-century bastioned walls, it has handed down to the modern eye the city-state of the Middle Ages. Almost intact, the city offers the modern visitor its finely spun web of medieval houses, towers and churches, densely packed together, set off against the stately palazzi and aristocratic townhouses of the Renaissance and 18th century.

It is in all likelihood thanks to its walls, which have remained intact throughout the course of centuries, that Lucca escaped the wanton destructive forces of the modern world which, in the name of sham «renewal», have caused the demise of artistically and historically important districts in other Italian cities since the last century.

Of the ancient Roman Lucca little remains, or has survived the ravages of time and the barbarian migrations save the Amphitheatre ruins, traces of wall segments and the still discernible quadrilateral urban layout. Sometime after the first millennium A.D., concomitant with the rea-

wakening in trade and industry and the rise of the communes or city-states of the Middle Ages, Lucca began to emerge from its ruins and build for the future. The 12th and 13th centuries were the age of builders, when a great many of the city's actual monuments were erected.

In the 1200s new walls arose, girding the ancient Roman nucleus that was now encircled within this perimeter by the recently completed city districts, distinct from it in plan. Adjacent to the Romanesque churches rose tall new tower-houses, which in turn punctuated the narrow winding lanes built-up with closely packed and equally new private dwellings, all of which are as typical of Lucca today as they were in the 13th-14th centuries. The pace of this development slowed considerably in the course of the next few centuries, a fact which is also attributable to internal strife among rival families and factions. This was a period of stabilisation within the city's walls, an epoch marked by the construction of new tower-houses in brick, with their inner courtyards and ground-floor log-gias and stores, next to the older ones of stone.

The lull in building during the 14th and 15th centuries gave way to a renewed boom in urban development in the Renaissance. The period was marked by relative peace and, in Lucca, coincided with a decided upsurge in trade and the arrival of new, wealthy families. From the 16th to the 18th centuries the old city — legacy of the Middle Ages — spreads beyond its enclave adding stately civic and private palazzi and erecting new municipal walls, incorporating areas that had until then been mere outskirts.

Following the tumultuous events of the French Revolution and its aftermath, Lucca and its interests cast their lot with the family of Napoleon. Fortune was good and the city prospered. The innovations, including the tree-lined thoroughfares along the bastions, the refurbishment of certain buildings, the construction of the spacious Piazza Napoleone and the long avenues laid out in the north-eastern sector, had the effect of transforming the city into an imperial court residence.

The lines along which Lucca developed through the centuries are distinctly discernible. They reveal a city of irreplaceable treasures, largely moulded in the likeness of the Middle Ages with roots extending to the world of antiquity; a city bejewelled by the finely cut stones of its Florentine-inspired Renaissance palazzi — some of which even today stand at the very centre of city politics and government. The fact that its urban development in the last century has taken place outside the historic walls is living testimony to the cultural and civic pride of the city and its institutions. With its Romanesque churches, medieval towers and dwellings, Renaissance palazzi and, of course, its famed walls, Lucca is a must for all discerning visitors.

Detail of the tomb of «Ilaria del Carretto».

Duomo (left). Dedicated to San Martino (St Martin), it was originally founded in the 6th century, subsequently renovated and thereafter completely refurbished to its final form in the 13th century. The Gothic interior with its central nave and flanking aisles is notable for the important works of art by Italian masters displayed throughout it.

Above: A revealing view of the interior and the majesty of the «Volto Santo» (Holy Countenance), a wooden crucifix from the 12-13th century and one of the most celebrated in all Italy, probably of eastern origin.

Below: «San Martino a Cavallo e il povero» (St Martin on Horseback and the beggar), Tuscan Romanesque sculpture set into the portico arches and supported by two ornate spandrels; and the tomb of «Ilaria del Carretto» (1408), a masterpiece by Jacopo della Quercia.

Above left: Aerial view of the city centre with a fine view from the Guinigi Tower. Centre: The ancient Arena, the layout of which is still visible. Below: Via dei Fossi, a typically picturesque street. Above: Side - view and holmoak - crowned tower of one of the Palazzi Guinigi, superbly decorated brick building of the late 14th century.

SAN FREDIANO (above). Built 1112-1147 on the site of a 6th-century basilica and subsequently raised in 1200 A.D., it still boasts its original architecture. The façade, stately yet simple in execution, is divided into three sections by two lesenes or pilaster-strips. The resulting triple portals are notable for their decorative motifs, the small loggia overhead and, above that, the magnificent mosaic of the Ascension (right). The interior, with its nave and aisles punctuated by columns crowned with medieval capitals, features prominent works of art. Right: «The Miracle of San Frediano» (1500) by Amico Aspertini.

SAN MICHELE (below). Built in the 12th century, it is a typical example of Pisan Lucchese architecture. The date 1143 is etched on the left abutment of the triumphal arch. The interior, laid out in a central nave set off from the side aisles by capital-headed columns, features a wealth of carvings, sculptures, frescoes and priceless paintings.

These are but a part of that body of works which gave form and structure to the surviving Roman town in the Middle Ages, and they have come down to us intact, as original today as they were then.

63

TOUR OF THE WALLS. Built from 1504-1645, the present walls are actually the third in order of historical appearance to be erected round Lucca. Extending 4195 metres, they were tree-lined and transformed into a public promenade during the epoch of Marie Louise de Bourbon in 1830. Above left: Trees along the walls. Below: interior of Paolino bulwark. Left: The medieval San Gervasio Gate (13th century) with its two towers. Right: An excellent view of the former Palazzo Controni (to-day Palazzo Pfanner) built in 1667. Adjoining it are the splendid garden and lawns the centre of which is adorned by a pond with a central fountain and numerous statues. Centre: Night view of the Teatro del Giglio during the Feast of St. Croce. Below: Villa Torrigiani at Camigliano.

BAGNI DI LUCCA

Noted summer resort and spa, the township includes such scenic outlying villages as Bagni Caldi and La Villa, hamlets situated along the banks of the Lima river amidst charming expanses of verdant wooden hills (see panorama). Its waters or baths, valued for their radioactivity and high temperature, have been known since the high Middle Ages, and their health-giving properties are attested to in documents dating to the 11th century. Bagni di Lucca enjoyed its moment of greatest splendour in the 19th century when, under the Napoleonic principality of Lucca and the governorship of the duke of Bourbon, it was regularly frequented by the Lucchese nobility and other illustrious European guests, among whom the writers and poets Montaigne, Byron, Shelley, Heine, d'Azeglio and Carducci have made mention of it in their writings. Above: Cocciglia ravine. The torrent has cut a deep gorge through time in the sheer rock. Centre: Houses along the Lima. Below: The «Ponte del Diavolo» (Devil's Bridge) at Mozzano.

BARGA

Located on a small rise in the Apennine foothills, it is one of the largest towns in the Serchio valley, although the exact date of its founding is obscure. Barga is two-tiered — a modern town in the flatland below and the old city above — with important industries and businesses and, most notable of all, a distinguished patrimony of medieval art and architecture.

Above: Two panoramas of Barga with its Cathedral. Right: «Il Ciocco», one of the most important and famous of Tuscany's international tourist resorts, site of many European-wide meets and events. Below: The home-cum-museum of the poet Giovanni Pascoli in the village of Colle di Caprone. The poet's burial monument by Plinio Novellini is located opposite the church of San Nicolò.

FORTE DEI MARMI

One of the most popular Tyrrhenian seaside resorts, it has excellent facilities and a wide swath of extra-fine sand that gently slopes into the sea. The town grew round the «Fortress» (left) which Leopold I ordered built in 1788, whence its name.

Today it is a modern and growing town with a happy air, fine palazzi and smart villas, and excellent tourist facilities. Framed by the silently dominating Apuan peaks rising behind it, Forte dei Marmi is further enhanced amidst its setting of pines.

68

Two views of the Apuan Alps (above): Monteforato (1223 m high) and Pania della Croce (1858 m high). Extending a thousand kilometres in length through the coastal lowlands, the Garfagnana and the inner Lunigiana, the Apuan chain reaches its highest summit at mount Pisanino, 1945 metres above sea level. These mountains are the world's leading source of marble, a fact which accounts for one of the landscape's most curious and startling facets. The bare rock left behind by the quariers is white, creating the impression from a distance that the mountains are snow-covered even in summer.

Views of Orecchiella State Park, 1250 metres above sea level (below, right). Situated in the Garfagnana near to the town of Castelnuovo di Garfagnana, it offers the visitor a splendid panorama of scenic beauty throughout the four seasons. It also offers the tourist an ideal haven for a bit of rest and relaxation.

VERSILIA

This is the 165-km-long coastal strip in northern Tuscany and is bounded in the east by the majestic and imposing ridge of the Apuan Alps, in the west by the Tyrrhenian Sea, in the north by the mouth of the Cinquale river and in the south by Lake Massaciuccoli.

Versilia's inland landscape features the ever-changing shapes of the hillsides, with their numerous vineyards and olive groves and thick woodlands, punctuated here and there by centuries-old towns and villages affording spectacular panoramas of the Tuscan riviera. Its coastline is crowned by beautiful stands of pine giving way to a long, almost perfectly straight littoral of picturesque beaches noted for their beauty and modern bathing facilities — among the most popular and «in» of these are Forte dei Marmi, Marina di Pietrasanta, Lido di Camaiore and Viareggio. To the south, below Viareggio, is magnificent Lake Massaciuccoli, and to the east the ridge of the Apuan Alps, protecting Versilia from the north winds and ensuring its climate remains mild. Versilia is ideal for summer holidays while affording just the right peace and quiet for a restful stay any time of the year.

VIAREGGIO

One of Europe's most well known sea and health resorts, Viareggio is a delightfully modern city set between two sprawling pine stands, its boulevards and linear streets bedecked with palms, oleanders and tamrasiks. Its elegant hotels, neat homes, shops and beautiful parks stand before a wide strip of fine sandy beach. The harbour's two piers jutting out a couple of hundred metres into the sea are perfect promenades from which strollers can enjoy splendid panoramic views of the coast — from Livorno (Leghorn) to La Spezia — and the towering peaks of the Apuan Alps.

70

Among the many cultural and artistic events at home here, the famous Carnival parade in costume and the Premio Viareggio for literature are the most famous.

While indeed catering to the tourist industry, Viareggio has managed to preserve its original seaport character. The large harbour is home to Tuscany's main commercial fishing fleet and to the many shipyards famous the world over for their pleasure craft.

Left: The boat basin against the backdrop of the gleaming and resplendent Apuan Alps. Below left: The Torre Matilde built by order of the Senate of Lucca in 1544. Right: Harbour canal and fishermen.

TORRE DEL LAGO PUCCINI

Of the two roads leading from this village, one takes you to the sea and the other, a linden-tree-lined boulevard of stately demeanor, runs to Lake Massaciuccoli and the picturesque villa overlooking it of Giacomo Puccini (1858-1924), who composed many of his operas here. One of the villa's rooms has been set aside as a chapel and contains his tomb.

Right: Lake Massaciuccoli; the linden-lined boulevard from Torre del Lago to Viareggio, a scene from «Tosca» staged during the opera season. Above: Giacomo Puccini.

73

MASSA

Nestled among the foothills of the Apuan Alps, it extends across the lowland as far as the shoreline. The old city is medieval to the core, having been built on a spur of rock and encircled by fortified walls. The upper part of the old city, called the Rocca (below left) was the princely residence of the Malaspinas. About this medieval enclave is modern Massa. Its growth is mainly a result of industrialization since the Second World War and tourism has caused such a sharp expansion in the residential districts (photo) that the town has developed along the roads leading to the industrial park zone and the coast where they have linked up with the port of Marina di Massa. Centre: Palazzo Cybo-Malaspina, today the seat of the Prefecture.

MARINA DI MASSA

A modern beach resort with ample accommodations, it also boasts elegant residential enclaves neatly arrayed amidst its pines. Its inviting beach is a wide strip about two kilometres in length. The Apuan Alps rising in the background keep the cold winds out and the temperate climate mild most of the year. A long straight road, with houses going up almost everywhere along it, links it to Massa. The local economy is largely the result of tourism and the marble industry.

Views: Panoramas of the inviting beaches.

CARRARA

Complacently set along the banks of the Torrente Carrione, it has spread unhurriedly over a large basin amidst the hillsides covered with olive groves and vineyards right up to the slopes of the Apuan Alps, the source of its beauty and world-wide renown. Carrara marble.

Albeit modern in appearance and outlook, the town has preserved in its centre the most important of its medieval monuments, the Duomo (11th-13th centuries) and Piazza Alberica. The quariers proper date to the Etruscans, who began to exploit them in earnest with the foundation of the town of Luni (7 Km distant) in 170

Left: An engaging panorama of the town. Below: 16th century palazzo built by order of Alberico I Cybo, today the site of the Academy of Fine Arts; and the Duomo, erected in the 11th century, apse enlarged in the 13th century, and refurbished in its present form in the 14th century. The Duomo's surface marble is in grey and white bands and the façade is Pisan Romanesque in style

B.C., although the Etruscans had already started working them sometime before. The Romans followed, adding the harbour for export of their valuable commodity. The quarriers subsequently became the property of the bishop of Luni, Pisa, Lucca, Parma, Milan and the Malaspina family. It is only in the 20th century, however, that Carrara becomes the world's foremost producer of commercial marble (mainly sculptural), an evolution that has provided the impetus needed for both the town and its industrial base to expand as far as Marina di Carrara and the coast. It is from the harbour of Marina di Carrara that the precious marble, excavated from the spectacular quarries of the Apuan Alps, is exported throughout the world.

Above: Before export, the marble is worked in this shop or «laboratory» by skilled hands trained at the local «marble school». Left: A sculptor at work.

MARINA DI CARRARA

Located at the northenmost edge of the Tyrrhenian Sea on the border with Liguria, it is a friendly and popular beach resort nestled at the foot of the Apuan Alps. Its large sandy swath is broken at the centre by the commercial harbour and its two piers from which the marble quarried at Massa is shipped.

Views: The harbour against the scenic background of the Apuan Alps and the beach.

79

PISA

History

Divided into two parts by the River Arno, Pisa lies only 4 metres above sea level on the fertile plain that extends from the foot of Monte Pisano to the coast, only 5 or 6 miles from the city centre.

With a population of only just over one hundred thousand, Pisa has a civil and military airport, is an archiepiscopal seat, and boasts a university of ancient historical and cultural traditions. The University of Pisa was founded, in fact, as long ago as the twelfth century, making it one of the oldest and most glorious of Italian universities. An agricultural and industrial centre of note, Pisa is well-linked to the rest of the peninsula: a main station on the Rome-Genoa line, it is also served by branch lines connecting it to Florence via Empoli or via Lucca and Montecatini Terme as well as to Siena. It is also an important main road and motorway junction. As a result the numerous resorts on the Tyrrhenian Sea and in the mountains are easily accessible, as are the thermal centres: S. Giuliano Terme is a mere 2 miles from the city, while Montecatini and Monsummano Terme are no more than 25-30 miles away.

As far as the climate is concerned, Pisa may be included among the most temperate zones of Italy. Sheltered from the cold north winds by Monte Pisano, the Garfagnana mountains and the Maritime Alps, its proximity to the coast allows it to breathe the warm winds from the west and the south. As a result the city, which offers a wide choice of hotel accommodation, is an ideal location for a pleasant stay and makes a good centre for excursions to the places mentioned above, not to mention others such as Lucca, Torre del Lago Puccini (the great composer's country house), Collodi with the Pinocchio Monument and its historical gardens, Livorno, etc.

Pisa, however, owes its fame principally to its ancient and noble past: it is said that it is older even than Rome, and in its time it was one of the most powerful of the Marine Republics.

There is a certain amount of disagreement with regard to the origins of the city, but one of the more reliable sources leads us to believe that it was probably founded between the fifth and seventh centuries B.C. It was at first a Greek colony founded by the Phoceans and later an Etruscan one. From 180 B.C. it was a Roman colony and Augustus named it «Colonia Julia Pisana». The fortunes of the city were always governed by the sea, which at that time arrived at the very gates of the city. Pisa first became a powerful Marine Republic in the eleventh century, after the period during which it was allied with the Romans up to the second Punic war, and after Caesar Octavian had established the harbour in a natural bay (the «Sinus Pisanus») at the estuary of the River Arno, where big ships could dock. Before this time the city had been under the Odoacer, the Ostrogoths, the Byzantines, the Longobards and Franks, then annexed to the Marquisate of Tuscany under the Carolingians.

As a powerful marine Republic, Pisa fought against the Saracens and conquered Corsica, Sardinia and the Balearic Islands; it asserted its high prestige also in the East, especially after having participated in the 1st Crusade. The problem now was to consolidate and maintain its influence over the conquered territories and consequently long and fierce struggles against Amalfi and Genoa for supremacy over land and sea were never lacking. Added to this

One of the splendid ceiling coffers in the Church of the Cavalieri: Jacopo Chimenti's Capture of Four Turkish Ships by Six Pisan Triremes in the Aegean Sea in 1602. Right, the historical Porta Nuova.

Aerial panorama of the Piazza dei Miracoli.

constant military effort there was strong internal unrest mainly caused by the Guelf-Tuscan league on account of speculation and contrast as to how the enormous amassed wealth was to be administrated. The result was that even though they managed to resist the Guelf city-states and the followers of Guelf amongst the citizens of Pisa, the city became slowly weaker, so much so that upon being engaged simultaneously, on the seas of Levant, in rivalry with the Republic of Venice, and on the Mediterranean against Genoa, it suffered a disastrous defeat by Genoa in the famous battle of Meloria in 1284. It was the «day of Saint Sistus», anniversary of many victories, but this time Pisa had lost. The Republic went on, but the glory, prestige and rule of the sea came to an end. In this manner, after an extraordinary adventure, the economic and political decline of Pisa started; broke down the free-city institutes and in their place the families of nobles asserted their authority: first came the Uguccione della Faggiola, then the Della Gherardesca and then the Gambacorta. Finally the D'Appiano ruled over the fortunes of Pisa until it passed to the Visconti, who ceded it to the authority of Florence in the year 1405.

Although Pisa had now lost its political independence, nevertheless, under the wise rule of the Medici, the town developed progressively as a cultural and intellectual centre. Cosimo the 1st de' Medici, for instance, renewed the study of the Sapienza. Leopoldo the 2nd reorganized the Scuola Normale Superiore founded by Napoleon in the year 1810.

After so many historical vicissitudes, in the year 1860, Pisa joined the Kingdom of Italy after a solemn plebiscite.

During the 2nd World War the town suffered considerable destruction from heavy bombing raids and because of the dogged resistance of the Germans on the opposite banks of the Arno River, just within the limits of town-walls. This resistance lasted 40 days. Casualties were very high and the destruction was not limited only to public property but also to artistic treasures. In the field of art the grand «Camposanto Monumentale» (Monumental Churchyard), the marble walls of which close off one side of the imposing «Piazza dei Miracoli», was seriously damaged.

THE CATHEDRAL

This grandiose masterpiece of Romanesque-Pisan Style was started in the year 1063 by the great architect Buschetto. It is, therefore, the first work undertaken in the spot that became later the «Piazza dei Miracoli». It was possible because of the enormous wealth amassed by the powerful Sea Republic which at that time Pisa was, particularly after having carried out a fruitful raid on Palermo. The Cathedral was consecrated in the year 1118, even though still incomplete, by Pope Gelasio the 2nd. It was finished in the 13th century, with the erection of the façade, unchanged up to today, by Rainaldo, who also built the main apse.

Duomo: Main façade door.

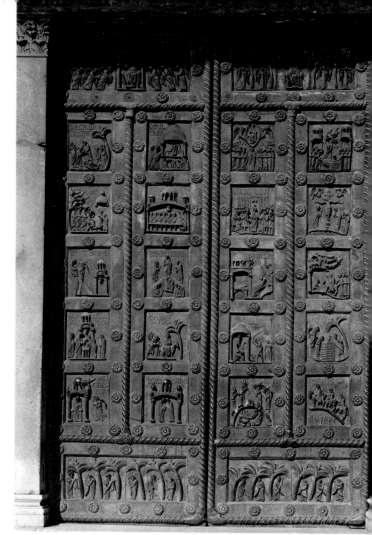

Duomo: San Ranieri Door (1180) by Bonanno Pisano.

The Cathedral, designed in Latin-Cruciform, basically has a romanesque architectural style, but at the same time interprets and absorbs elements of the styles of various periods, thus forming a unique style which has something of the sublime. The Cathedral was adorned, a little at a time through the years, with numerous works of art. It is undoubtedly Giovanni Pisano who excels in these works, especially for his famous, extremely rich and ingenious Pergamo (Pulpit).

For a brief idea of its dimensions the Cathedral is one hundred meters long. The façade is 35.40 mts wide. It is 34.20 mts high; hence both imposing and of an ingenious and grandiose conception.

THE FAÇADE OF THE CATHEDRAL

The façade of the cathedral is articulated in five rows of arches, the lowest of which has seven blind arches, two lateral and one central door, separated by columns and coupled pilasters. In the year 1595 a furious fire broke out and destroyed these doors (as well as the ceiling and other works on the inside); the present doors are thus not the original ones of the master Bonanno, but those made by the artists of the school of Giambologna - Francavilla, Mocchi, Tacca.

The central door depicts the life of Mary. The two lateral ones represent the life of the Redeemer. Still in this bottom row the walls are decorated with numerous tarsia-rose-windows, grooves, inlays of ornamental glass and geometrical panels to give a sense of grace and refinement.

The upper rows present open-galleries that contrast with the walls giving depth and movement so that the massive proportions of the whole façade become refined and at the same time rendered precious by a fine and elaborate fretwork.

Above the central gate, there is a memorial inscription to Rainaldo. The sarcophagus of Buschetto, who started the construction of the cathedral, lies in the first arcade to the left. On the top of the façade, there is a statue of the Madonna of Andrea Pisano and at the sides angels of the School of Giovanni Pisano. At both sides of the first order of galleries there are the statues of two evangelists. The whole cathedral, both on the two sides and in the apses, repeats the decorative and ornamental themes of the façade, albeit with slight differences. Also here are repeated the polychrome-tarsias, grooved panels, inlays of coloured glass. The whole cathedral is wonderful work of architecture and sculpture not at all lacking in grace in spite of its stately and massive conception.

The ovoidal dome, raised over the main body of the cathedral where it is crossed by the transept, is of Gothic style.

THE INTERIOR OF THE CATHEDRAL

In order to appreciate the full majesty of the building, the visitor is advised first of all to go to the inner wall of the cathedral façade (at the furthest end from the St.

Duomo: Coffered ceiling and Galileo's chandelier.

Duomo: Galileo Galilei's chandelier.

Ranieri door, the usual point of entry). The complete view that may be enjoyed from this point is such as to convey a deep, religious feeling, to which is added a sense of bewilderment as we contemplate the vast spaces of the building and the grandeur of its architecture and its sculptures: it is almost as if not the hand of man but the divine will had created that which lies spread before us.

From the middle of this wall, looking down the nave, our attention is drawn to the long, suggestive line of the imposing granite colonnades — almost all of them original — with their Corinthian capitals, and then to the women's gallery with its little loggias located above the nave, to the rich, highly decorated lacunar ceiling, and to the deep terminal apse from which the figure of Christ enthroned stands out, commanding our attention. Everything, including the play of the minor colonnades and the black and white panels which line the walls, play their part in adding vivacity and a sense of movement to the grandiose conception of the building.

Let us now pass to its description and to the visit. Internally it is divided into five aisles, a central major aisle flanked by two minor ones on each side. The transept has three aisles. Against the second line of columns of the central nave there are two holy water founts. The statues on these depict, on one side, Jesus and on the other side St. John the Baptist (17th century, by F. Palma).

◀ *Duomo: Interior.*

THE PULPIT

We are before a work of rare richness, if not, indeed, one of the great masterpieces of all time. The plasticity of the sculptures in this work seems animated by an emotive tension that is almost dramatic in its conception.

While Nicola Pisano, Giovanni's father, in his Pulpit in the Baptistry, for instance, expresses himself with the religious gravity characteristic of the Romanesque period, his son Giovanni, in his work in the Cathedral with which we are now concerned, has broken away completely from the carefully considered, almost cold reproduction of the earlier style, giving his figures life and breath and animating them with a deeply human sense.

The pulpit with its hexagonal base, work of Giovanni Pisano (1302-1311), is located near the first pillar of the vault. In the year 1599 it was dismantled and rebuilt only in the year 1926. It rests on eleven columnar supports that in turn rest on lions and on pedestals. Other supports are represented by statues of St. Michael, Hercules, the Evangelists supporting Christ and «The four Cardinal virtues» which support the Church. The central support represents «The Arts of the Trivium and Quadrivium». The capitals of the supports are sculptured with figures of Sibyls. In the lateral corbels there are Evangelists and Prophets. A cornice separates the section described above from the panels composing the upper portion of the pulpit and the figures of Prophets and Saints that are located between the panels. In the panels are dramatically rep-

Duomo: St Agnes by Andrea del Sarto.

Duomo: The Virgin and Child by G. Sogliano (16th century).

resented the events preceding and following Christ's birth. They are:

1) Annunciation - Visitation - Birth of St. John the Baptist.

2) Birth of Jesus Christ.

3) The Wise Kings.

4) Presentation at the temple and the flight into Egypt.

5) The slaughter of the innocents.

6) The kiss of Judas - The arrest of Christ - The scourging of Christ.

7) The crucifixion.

8) The chosen one.

9) The reprobates.

At this point the visit can be considered ended and it only remains to glance once more around the whole edifice and then to go out on to the vast lawn «of the miracles».

Duomo: The famous depiction of the Four Cardinal Virtues: Justice with scales and sword, Temperance holding the cornucopia and compass, Fortitude holding the lion by the legs, and Prudence naked. Superimposed on the group is the figure of the Church symbolised by a woman nursing two infants who probably stand for the Old and New Testaments (detail of the Pulpit).

Duomo: The Pulpit (1302-1311) by Giovanni Pisano. ▶

Poster, inside pages: Two views of the Leaning Tower and a giant aerial panorama of Piazza dei Miracoli.

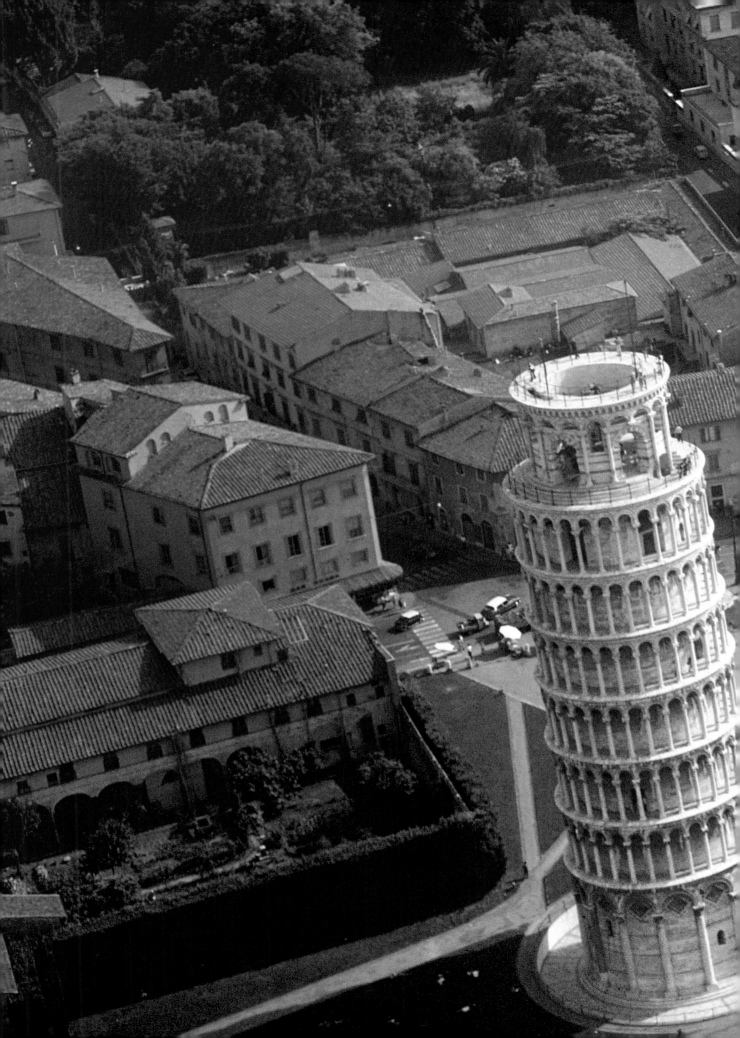

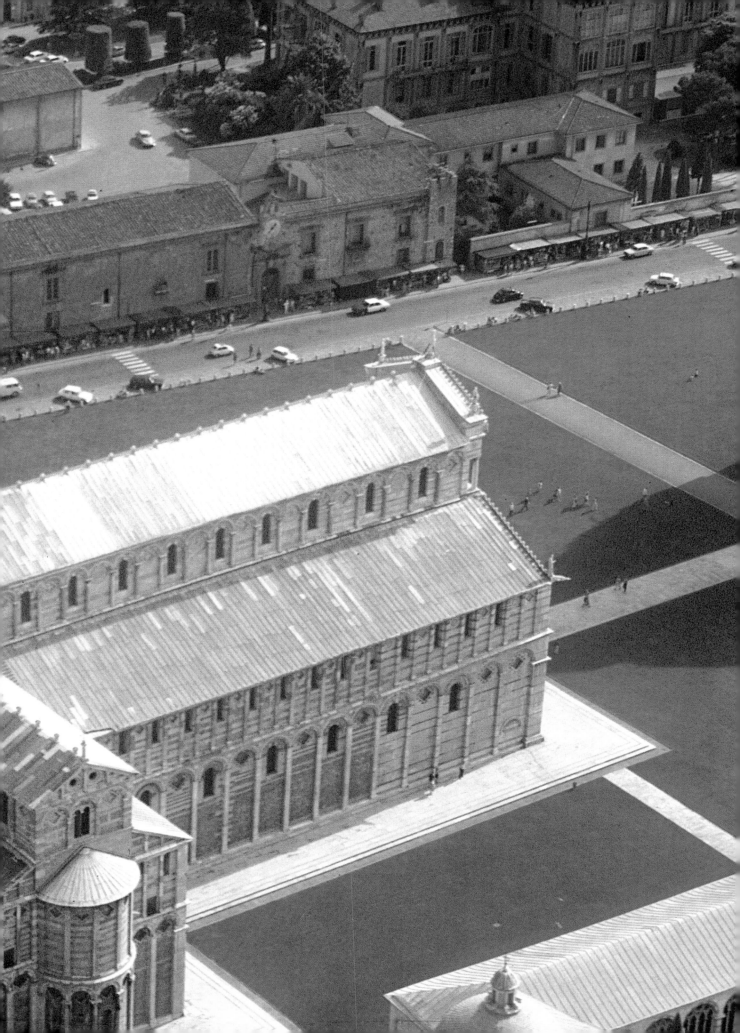

THE LEANING TOWER

Above: Bas-relief at the Tower's base with the date the building began. Below: Romanesque capital. Above, right: The sixth order of small loggias and the belfry. Below: The Tower seen in full inclination.

This is the monument which, more than any other in the Piazza dei Miracoli, stirs the imagination of everybody, young and old alike.

First of all some historical information. The construction of this imposing edifice was begun in the year 1174 by Bonanno Pisano. When construction had reached the third storey, work was suspended as a result of subsidence and the tower remained incomplete for around 90 years, until it was completed after 99 years by Giovanni di Simone. Tommaso, son of Andrea Pisano, crowned the tower with the belfry.

The top of the Leaning Tower can be reached by mounting the 294 steps which rise in the form of a spiral on the inner side of the tower walls.

The tower is 55.863 mts high.

Max height 56.705 mts.

The inside diameter at the base is 7.368 mts.

The outer diameter at the base is 15.484 mts.

The inclination is 4.551 mts.

There are 8 storeys.

It is supported by foundations about 3 mts. deep.

The Tower weighs about 14,500 tons.

In the belfry there are 7 bells, each one corresponding to a note of the musical scale.

The oldest bell is that named «Pasquareccia» which rang to announce that the Earl Ugolino della Gherardesca, sentenced for treachery, was starving to death together with his sons and grandsons in the tower of Piazza delle Sette Vie (today Piazza dei Cavalieri). On the top of the tower Galileo Galilei carried out famous experiments including that regarding the effects of gravity. It is one of the seven wonders of the world. From the top we can enjoy a vast view that, starting from Monte Pisano, the mountains of Garfagnana and the Apuan Mountains slopes down towards us, revealing the great extent of the whole fertile plain which, before reaching the sea, meets the grandiose and extensive forest regions of Migliarino and S. Rossore.

ART OF THE TOWER

This very famous work is of Romanesque style and, as already stated, dates back to the year 1174. Cylindrical in shape it demonstrates externally six open galleries. A cornice separates these galleries one from the other and each presents a series of small arches fitted on the capitals of the slender columns. In the base there is a series of big blind arcades, between which elaborate, geometrical designs have been executed. In the belfry the arcades are continued as in the base, with the difference that here, apart from the reduced proportions, there are apertures or doors for the movement of the bells.

Although imposing, this monument is not lacking in elegance and lightness due to the effect of the arcades and open galleries between one storey and another. The entrance is surmounted by a lunette on which is sculptured a work of Andrea Guardi, the «Madonna and child, St. Peter and St. John».

Although it may be considered a masterpiece of architecture, the tower is famous mainly for the way in which it leans. There is no doubt that this phenomenon is the result of land subsidence right from the time of its construction: the idea that it was intentionally built in this way is entirely without foundation. Unfortunately, even today the great mass continues to sink very slowly. It is a question of about 1 mm, every year. Since nobody can state with mathematical certainty that this sinking effect will continue in the future at the present annual rate without ceasing, remedies by means of adequate measures, based on scientific studies and projects, are under consideration. In the meantime supervision of the phenomenon with instruments of very high precision is continuously being carried out.

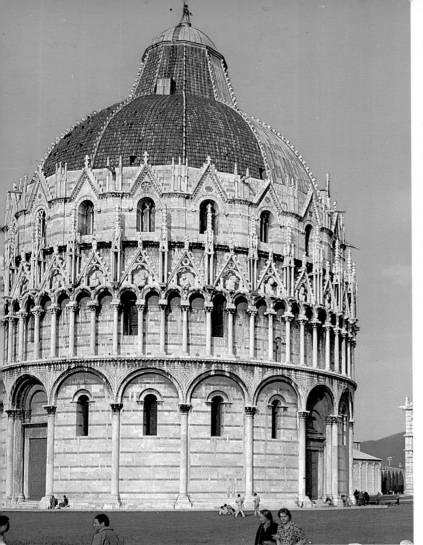

THE BAPTISTRY

Located in front of the Cathedral façade, the construction of this great building was begun in the year 1 under the direction of the architect Diotisalvi, as is sta on an epigraph to be found on a pillar inside the monument. It was thus the second monument to rise in piazza — work on the church bell tower (the fam «Leaning Tower») was begun many years later, in 11 Like the other monuments in the Piazza dei Mira work on the Baptistry progressed slowly, with many terruptions. In fact, it was only in 1260 that work got under way with any real alacrity under Nicola Pis after an interruption of many years. The work was fir completed as late as the end of the 14th century un the direction of Cellino di Neve and Zimbellino Bologn

The Baptistry has a circular base, and is of three or (or stories) surmounted by a dome rising from the order (or Tambour). The height of this imposing buil is 55 metres and its diameter is 35.5 metres. It has doors, the main one opening towards the façade of Cathedral. Despite its vast mass, its appearance is tened by the rich variety of its numerous Gothic d rations.

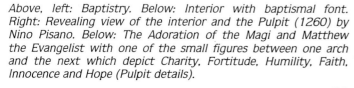

*Above, left: Baptistry. Below: Interior with baptismal font.
Right: Revealing view of the interior and the Pulpit (1260) by
Nino Pisano. Below: The Adoration of the Magi and Matthew
the Evangelist with one of the small figures between one arch
and the next which depict Charity, Fortitude, Humility, Faith,
Innocence and Hope (Pulpit details).*

99

The Monumental Camposanto: Façade and main entrance.

Camposanto: Interior.

THE MONUMENTAL CEMETERY

Coming out of the baptistry and looking once more at the majestic façade of the cathedral one will see to the left the churchyard which presents its long marble walls in the form of a rectangle. These boundary walls are composed of blind-arcades on pilasters similar to those of the cathedral, tower and baptistry just visited. In these walls there are two entrances in the arcades. The main gate is the one on the right next to the cathedral, over which stands a Gothic three-cusped tabernacle with «Madonna and Saints». It is a work of Giovanni Pisano and his school.

Before passing over to a description of other things, it should be mentioned that the churchyard is a work that dates back to about the end of the 13th century and was started by Giovanni di Simone. Centuries passed before it was completed, just as for the other monuments of the square.

It is said that the archbishop Ubaldo de' Lanfranchi, in 1203, brought earth from the Golgotha Mountain with galleys coming back from a crusade, because it seems that this earth was capable of reducing a body into a skeleton within twenty four hours. When Giovanni di Simone began work the churchyard already existed. In fact, the aim of this monumental work as started by him was to gather within a limited area in an orderly and dignified

100

THE TRIUMPH OF DEATH

The scene represents a riding party who are going hunting. The group consists of powerful nobles, ladies of the court and knights with their trail of helpers, arm-carriers, game and dogs. The party stops in front of three open coffins containing the remains of the King. Alongside is Macarius, an anchorite saints who is intent on teaching the party how life is vain when confronted with the reality, although disturbing but true, of the Triumph of Death. For her, we are all equal: power, vanity, wealth have no meaning and nor does the social level to which one belons.

manner all the graves scattered around the cathedral and at the same time to leave space for others in the future, in accordance with the deep rooted tradition of the noble families of Pisa of this time.

101

PIAZZA DEI CAVALIERI

After the «Piazza dei Miracoli» we would suggest starting the visit of the town from the «Piazza dei Cavalieri», not only because it is the most important and beautiful square, after that of the cathedral, but also because it is nearby. Leaving the cathedral and entering the old Via S. Maria and proceeding along Via dei Mille, we come out at Piazza dei Cavalieri. We find here a group of buildings that surrounds it irregularly but at the same time with an extraordinary harmony. We notice at once the Palace of the Knight's Caravan (after which the square is named), now occupied by the High School. Beyond that, we see the National Church of St. Stephen of the Knights. The Clock Palace is on the left of the entrance of the Via dei Mille. On the opposite side of the Clock Palace, there is the Palace of Puteano College and the Council Palace of the Order of St. Stephen. The fountain locat-ed in the square is a work of the year 1596 of P. Francavilla. Near it is the statue of Cosimo the 1st de' Medici, who founded the Order of the Knights of St. Stephen.

NATIONAL CHURCH OF ST. STEPHEN OF THE KNIGHTS

This is a work of the 16th century of Vasari who, later, also built the bell-tower in 1572. The church presents a marble façade by Don Giovanni de' Medici (1606) with a single portal in the middle, above which is the Emblem of the Knights' Order. Flanking the sides of the church are two wings that were once used as dressing-rooms for the knights of the order of St. Stephen. These were later transformed into two aisles of the church by Pier Francesco Silvani.

THE INTERIOR is formed of a nave with an extremely beautiful wooden inlaid ceiling. In each of the six portions, into which it is divided, is a painting representing «The glory of the knights». These works are of C. Allori, Empoli, Ligozzi and Cigoli.

On entering the church we can admire the two precious holy water founts of Vasari while, on the right and left hand wall, we see high up between the windows, four ship lanterns. These same walls are hung with tapestries and flags captured from the Turks. In this church there are also figureheads of ships of the Order of St. Stephen. Still on the wall we see four distempers (two on each side) representing «Episodes of St. Stephen's Life», by Vasari, Empoli, Allori and Ligozzi. To be noted also is the small but precious marble pulpit of the year 1627 of C. Fancelli. The walls of the church have four doors — two on both sides — which open into the two aisles that, as previously mentioned, were used as dressing rooms for the Knights of St. Stephen.

In the right aisle at the first altar we see the «Lapida-

The monument to Cosimo I dei Medici by Francavilla.

tion of St. Stephen» of G. Vasari. At the second altar there is a crucifix by Tacca. In the left aisle at the first altar, near the exit of the church, there is «The miracle of the loaves and fishes» of Buti; at the second altar the «Nativity of Jesus», the work of Bronzino.

At the high altar there is the sarcophagus of St. Stephen Pope (P.F. Silvani and Giovan Battista Foggini, 1700). Behind the altar a gilt bronze bust of «St. Lussorio» of Donatello is preserved within a glass-bell.

Of the palaces which surround the square let us dwell for a moment upon the one that is today occupied by the High School, Vasari's 16th century renovation of the old Palace of the Elders of the Pisan Republic. This building was appointed by Cosimo the 1st de' Medici to receive the military order of the knights of St. Stephen, hence it was also called «Palace of the Caravan». Observe the originality of the building, its slight curvature with a graffito-decorated façade, and the series of busts of the Grand Dukes of Tuscany of that time at the second storey and in the middle, above a balcony, the escutcheon of the Medici family.

Moving over to the Palace of the Clock, we can admire the originality of the successful architectural re-utilization of two ancient towers from designs of Vasari, The Gualandi (or Gherardesca) tower and that of the Municipal Jail, known as the Torre delle Sette Vie. It was in the Gualandi tower that Count Ugolino della Gherardesca was imprisoned, together with his sons and grandsons, on a

Piazza dei Cavalieri. Left: Palazzo della Gherardesca with the Muda Tower and Palazzo dei Cavalieri.

charge of high treason, and starved to death. Count Ugolino was at that time Podestà of the town and the Marine Republic of Pisa had just suffered a clamorous defeat at sea by the Republic of Genoa in the famous battle of Meloria (1284).

Also of note are the Puteano Palace of the 17th century and the Palace of the Council of the Order (Francavilla 1603), then seat of the Law-Court of St. Stephen's Order and today seat of the High School for applied sciences «A. Pacinotti».

Church of Santo Stefano dei Cavalieri.

Santo Stefano dei Cavalieri: Interior. Below, left: Bust of San Rossore (or San Lussorio), an exceptional reliquary in gilded bronze set in the choir behind the church's altar. Below: The splendid coffered ceiling of wood inlay superbly decorated. The six coffers commemorate the deeds of the Cavalieri. This one, the work of Jacopo da Empoli, depicts the razing of Bona in 1607.

CHURCH OF SANTA MARIA DELLA SPINA

This jewel of Gothic art of Pisan-style is located on the Lungarno Gambacorti. Initially it was an oratory at the extreme limit of the Arno River. After it was enlarged by Lupo Capomaestro in 1323 and named Chiesa della Spina (church of the thorn) because it preserved one of the thorns of the Christ crown. In the year 1871, after about five hundred years, the church was dismantled piece by piece and rebuilt in a safer location away from the river waters that had badly damaged it. This very beautiful small church is covered with an extremely rich marble decorations of gentle contrasting colours and a suggestive series of cusps and pinnacles.

THE OLD STRONGHOLD

Facing the Lungarno as it runs alongside the church of S. Paolo a Ripa d'Arno and the square of the same name, we can admire the ancient Fortress of Pisa which is reflected in the waters of the river. When the sky behind the fortress is scattered with clouds tinted different hues by the setting sun, the effect is quite breathtaking. This fortress of the old city was rebuilt and enlarged by the Florentines who conquered Pisa in the 15th century. In 1558 Ferdinando I de' Medici built a shipyard for the construction of galleys of the Order of St. Stephen. It was heavily damaged in 1944 by the ravages of the war.

THE CAMPANO TOWER

The «Campano» (big bell), situated near the market, is so-called because of the enormous size of its bell, made so as to be heard even in the most distant parts of the city and surrounding country. In this way, students were reminded that school lessons were about to begin.

ILLUMINATION OF ST. RANIERI

This takes place every year on the evening of the 16th June along the Lungarni. For this occasion the Leaning Tower is also illuminated. It is a phantasmagoric candlelight-illumination of the beautiful medieval palaces along the Lungarni, that so lighted reproduce fantastic reflections in the waters of the river, where at the same time hundreds of flickering lights slowly float down towards the sea. This sight, which draws thousands of townspeople and tourists, is crowned by a spectacular fireworks display. This spectacle is in honour of the patron Saint of the town, whose feastday recurs the day after, on the 17th of June.

HISTORICAL REGATTA OF ST. RANIERI

Held on 17th June, feast of the Patron Saint of the town, in the Arno River with crews in costume manning antique style boats. People representing various quarters of the town take part in this game.

THE MONASTERY OF PISA

Located in fertile country among the valleys with their olive-trees and vineyards where peace and silence reign absolute, it was founded in the year 1366 and comprises church, cloisters, cells of the Carthusians and guest-rooms. There are a number of works of a certain artistic importance and interest, but the visitor will be mostly impressed by the charm of the late-baroque style of the white buildings, rich in marbles, contrasting with the green of the surrounding countryside to create an atmosphere of elegance and at the same time a sense of the religious most appropriate to the setting. The tourist, after his visit to the Carthusian Monastery of Pisa, should not omit a visit to the Romanesque Parish Church of Calci, founded at the end of the 11th century with its urn inside the high-altar containing the relics of Saint Ermolao, Patron Saint of the valley. The remains were placed in this church in the year 1111 by the Archbishop of Pisa Pietro Moriconi.

BASILICA ROMANA ST. PETER AT GRADO

The origin of this ancient basilica is tied to a legend. In 1800 Da Morrona wrote: «St. Peter, on arriving from Antioch and when landing along the Tuscan shore, in a place called Grado, so named because of the steps, washed by the waves, where the boats landed, judged it an appropriate place for raising the first altar and temporarily founding a church». During recent excavations in fact, an ancient church of the 6th century was discovered under the present one, which was constructed in the 12th century.

The work is of Romanesque style, has four apses and is made of tuff.

SAN MINIATO

Laid out atop three knolls facing the Arno valley (see panoramic view), San Miniato is at once striking yet graceful in appearance and is renowned for its wealth of art treasures. Originally built round a nucleus consisting of an 8th-century church dedicated to this Florentine martyr, the town had already become the seat of the Vicariate by the reign of Otto I (the Great, 936-973 A.D.). Among the vicars to reside there was Boniface, Marquis of Tuscany and father of the Countess Mathilda. It also served as the home of Frederick I Barbarossa, Henry IV, Otto IV and Frederick II, who had the fort built in 1240.

Palazzo dei Vicari dell'Imperatore (Palace of the Emperor's Vicars). One of San Miniato's most prominent buildings both historically and architecturally, it was completed in the 11th-12th centuries and at one time included the crenellated tower (below) among its most interesting features. It was the residence of Boniface III, and Mathilda (1046-1115) almost certainly lived here. The Duomo (centre). Built in the 13th century, it features three Cinquecento (16th century) doors in stylistic harmony, an imposing bell tower familiarly called Mathilda's Tower (fig. 25), and an interior laid out in a Latin-cross plan with nave and columned aisles.

VOLTERRA

Perched atop the highest hill at the juncture of the Era and Cecina valleys, Volterra looks down from its solitary aerie upon a wide vista of surrounding hills. The town's importance through the ages had been primarily linked to its metal resources, the mainstay of the economy.

The Etruscans called it Velathri, and, from one of their oldest settlements, it rose to become in the 4th-5th centuries B.C. one of the leading members of the League of 12 Cities (locumonie) presiding over the fortunes of Etruria. Its walls, erected during this same period, extended over 7 kms, with an estimated 25 000 people living within them. In due course, Volterra came to dominate Populonia, Elba, Corsica, and the entire Tyrrhenian coast as far north as Luni in Versilia.

Left: Palazzo dei Priori (1208). The oldest of the medieval Communes or city halls extant in Tuscany, it casts an imposing presence on the visitor. Above: a picturesque street and Palazzo dei Priori. Right: Porta dell'Arco, one of the most important remnants of the town's original Etruscan walls; the Medici fortress, next the 14th-century Rocca Vecchia, was erected after 1472 by order of Lorenzo «il Magnifico». Below: The Balze and Badia, a striking image attesting to the precarious geological shifts that have recently begun to affect the town.

111

By virtue of its geographical position and its vast holdings, Volterra was one of the last Etruscan cities to capitulate to the power of Rome. When it did succumb, joining the Italic Confederation in 260 B.C., it did so on its own terms, being allowed to retain a certain autonomy and privileges.

Medieval Volterra. Built from the 12th to the 13th centuries inside the Etruscan walls, its old centre comprising the 13th-century Duomo and Piazza dei Priori is practically intact today.

From the 15th century onward, the town's history reflects the ebb and flow of the events about it. Drawn into the wars and conflicts of rival Tuscan cities it was contested by both Siena and Florence, with the latter finally securing it for both its strategic value and mineral resources. Thereafter, annexed to Florence by decree in 1411, Volterra was bound to the fortunes of the Duchy of Florence and the Grand Duchy of Tuscany. Today this community of farmers and tradesmen can draw upon the skilled alabaster craftsmen and a conspicuous tourist trade to bolster its economy. Most important is the Guernacci Museum with its rich collection of Etruscan works of art.

Museo Etrusco Guernacci (Guernacci Etruscan Museum): Funeral urns with covers dating to the Hellenistic period (3rd-1st centuries BC).

LIVORNO

Situated at the southernmost end of the Arno flood plain, Leghorn is today a modern city, having been extensively rebuilt following the widespread destruction suffered during World War II. The largest harbour on the Tyrrhenian and one of the biggest in all Italy, the city is a leading centre of trade, shipbuilding, metal working, machine plants, oil refineries and chemical plants.

The first mention made of Leghorn is in documents dated 904 A.D., where it is referred to as «Livorna», a fishing hamlet under the control of Porto Pisano. Fortified by the Pisans in 1392 amid a general defensive bolstering of Porto Pisano itself, it was ceded to the Visconti of Milan, then sold in 1405 to the Genoese who subsequently handed it over to the Medicis of Florence in 1421.

The city's fortunes were from then on closely linked to the rule of the Medicis who, in the latter 16th century, adopted a series of measures improving the port's facilities and making it the most important commercial harbour in Tuscany. Further development was spurred by special customs duties and the arrival of numerous foreign merchants many of whom were Jews. Thus, by the 1700s, Leghorn had become Tuscany's second city in both importance and size.

Following annexation to the Kingdom of Italy, the city embarks upon an era of unprecedented growth. Hardworking and astute, the Livornese are quick to exploit their opportunities and, soon, industry and tourism join ranks with the more traditional trade activities. Since its founding in 1881, the renowned Italian Naval Academy has been located here as well.

Leghorn today has a street plan that plainly reveals the scars left by the demolitions in the old city at the start of this century and the devastation wrought by the last world war. The old core of the Medici era with its surrounding Fossi or moat-works, built by order of Francesco I round the medieval castle overlooking the water and completed in 1577, has retained the original geometric layout of its streets but has lost many of its monuments. The most important of those that survive are the «Monumento Ai Quattro Mori» (Monument to the Four Moors), one of the city's most famous works of art, the Venezia Quartiere or district, the two fortresses and several churches and palazzi.

Piazza Grande and The Duomo (left). Standing in the heart of the old city and surrounded by modern buildings and porticos, they both had to be completely rebuilt after the bombing in 1943. Centre: The City Hall. Erected in 1720 and designed by Giovanni del Fantasia, it features a prominent double stairway in marble at the base of the façade. Below: Terrazza Mascagni, beautiful and modern, next to Palazzo Mascagni, housing the city aquarium.

Right: Piazza Giuseppe Micheli and its monument to Ferdinando I, popularly referred to as the «Four Moors». The statue of the grand duke (1595) is by Giovanni Bandini, and the Four Moors, added in 1626, at its base, by Pietro Tacca. Centre: Typical view along the Corso del Fosso Reale (Royal Moat Avenue), once the moat defending the Medici city bastions.

114

Below: Glimpse of Fortezza Vecchia. The city's largest monument, the imposing fortress was erected by order of Giulio de' Medici in 1521 and includes the massive tower (9th century A.D.) built by the marquises of Tuscany and the surrounding fort (1377), both of which predate it. The fortress features three bastions and two main entrances. Below: Detail, «Quattro Mori», and view of the Quartiere Venezia and the Fortezza Nuova, the latter having been built by order of the Medicis in 1590 on the marshes of the old Pisano port and originally linked to the Fortezza Vecchia.

Naval Academy: Hoisting the flag.

Naval Academy: The Brigantine.

NAVAL ACADEMY

Left: The Naval Academy Building (1878). Founded in 1881 by General Benedetto Brin, corps of naval engineers, the Academy educates and trains the future offi-

cers of the Italian Navy. It is also famous for the masted training ship Amerigo Vespucci, one of the most beautiful sailing vessels of its kind in the world. Right: Leghorn's barrier rocks and Galefuria tower fortress.

Naval Academy: Training ship Amerigo Vespucci at sea.

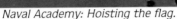

Naval Academy: Training ship Amerigo Vespucci in port.

Seaside bathing has been a tradition in Leghorn and the surrounding areas for over a hundred years. The Pancaldi Acquaviva, 1846, were the first beach facilities in what would become in time an important element in the local economy.

Left: Panorama of Castiglioncello. Alongside Marina di Campolecciano, Portovecchio and Coletta, it is one of the most attractive summer holiday areas in Tuscany, with beaches of sand and rock framed by lush vegetation. Above: Santuario di Montenero. Set on Montenero (black mountain), the shrine to the Madonna makes a fine day excursion affording a magnificent panorama of the Tyrrhenian. Adjacent: Cappella di San Guido (1703). A modest, simple structure, this octagonal chapel near Forte Bibbona and Bolgheri is immortalised in Carducci's ode «Davanti a San Guido» (Before St Guido).

118

POPULONIA

Founded by the Etruscans of Volterra as a colony on the coast of the Maremma, it is a raised site encircled by walls. Its period of greatest splendour came in the 7th century B.C., when trade with Greece was at its height. Ruled by Rome from the 3rd century B.C. on, it was continually beleaguered by attack and plundering through the succeeding centuries until ultimate decline quelled its slow agony.

Populonia today is noted especially for its archaeological sites which have helped scholars shed much light on the mysterious origins and history of the Etruscans.

Two views of the Etruscan necropolis and the medieval castle with its crenellated tower.

119

THE ISLE OF ELBA

The largest and most important island in the Tuscan archipelago, Elba lies about 10 Kms from the mainland opposite the gulf of Follonica across the Canale (channel) of Piombino. Vaguely triangular in form, it is 27 Km long — from Punta Nera to Capo Ortano — and 18 Km wide — from Capo della Vita to Punta dei Ripalti. Stretching 147 Km, its irregular coastline is marked by sheer rock cliffs, sandy coves and small bays which have made the island a favourite among European tourists.

Inland the isle is mountainous, with Monte Capanne at 1019 metres above sea level being the highest peak. On a clear sunny day you can see all six islands that make up the archipelago.

But let's get back to Elba, with its lush, typically Mediterranean vegetation, and its mild sea-sheltered temperate climate (never, not even in winter, does it go below 9°C (487°F). The island's economy is based on agriculture — prickly-pears, agave, palm, vineyards and olives, all in abundance — fishing, mining and tourism. Administratively under the province of Livorno, Elba comprises eight townships — Portoferraio, Campo nell'Elba, Capoliveri, Marciana, Marciana Marina, Porto Azzurro, Rio Marina and Rio nell'Elba.

PORTOFERRAIO

This snug harbour was already known to the Etruscans, who used to ship out the iron and copper bound for Populonia from here. From 260 B.C., with the arrival of the Romans, the little port merely changed hands rather than destiny. Let's say that the town itself really comes into being as such about 1548 under Cosimo I de' Medici; and, from 1814 to 1815, it was home to Napoleon. Views: Panorama, the harbour and Napoleon's villa.

San Martino - Napoleon's villa - La Paolina.

Its history is one of successive dominion. In antiquity, the Latins are already to be found here by 1000 B.C.; the Greeks arrive next (10th-6th centuries B.C.), drawn by the iron deposits. Thereafter, the Etruscans (6th century B.C.) from Populonia, who begin the systematic exploitation of the iron mines, and then the Romans, who began to quarry the excellent granite as well as mine the iron. From the Middle Ages onward, this pattern continued — first the Spanish, followed by the Pisans, the Florentines, Tuscans and, finally, Napoleon, who lived here from 3rd May 1814 to 26th February 1815. The last act in this odyssey of rulers was Elba's annexation — in 1815 to the Grand Duchy of Tuscany and in 1860 to the Kingdom of Italy.

MARCIANA MARINA

A typical fishing village with inlet, it is a very popular beach today. At the beginning of the jetty rises a tower which was built by the Pisans in the 12th century. View: Panorama, including the village and port.

Centre: A picturesque view of the coast from Capo d'Enfola.

MARINA DI CAMPO

An excellent beach resort with modern facilities, it was built on the beautiful, clearwater Golfo (gulf) di Campo. The seat of the Comune (township) di Campo dell'Elba, it features the imposing Medici Torre (tower), which dominates the crescent beach from its height on the granite promontory.

View: Marina di Campo's fishermen.

121

Piazza del Campo shaped like a sea shell, the Palazzo Pubblico and the Mangia Tower.

SIENA
History

It would seem that the foundation of Siena can be attributed to no less than the sons of one of the founders of Rome: Remus. On the death of their father, it seems that the two boys, Aschius and Senus, distrustful of their uncle Romulus, decided to flee from Rome. But they were poor and did not even have a horse on which to escape. They entreated Apollo to help them, promising to erect a temple to him in return. Their request was granted: two horses, one white and one black, appeared seemingly from nowhere. The boys mounted the two fiery steeds which galloped away without stopping until they had covered some 230 kilometres. When they did stop, the boys dismounted and the first thing they did was to erect the temple. Then they thought of a house for themselves. And so Siena was born.

Who knows if this is really what happened; it is certain, however, that the name of the city is very similar to the name of one of Remus's sons. Some think, less romantically, that the name Siena is derived from the Senonian Gauls, or Senese, who were the founders. But the fact that the city's coat of arm includes a she-wolf leads us to think that the Sienese prefer to consider themselves as Remus's heirs.

A rapid excursion into Siena's history: a Roman colony, it was converted to Christianity towards the end of the fourth century. It underwent sieges and invasions and, in the XI century, after being under the rule of the Carolingians, passed to the Bishops under whom it remained for less than 100 years when the Consuls gained the upper hand, giving the city new life. Siena, favouring the Ghibellines, knew great splendour in that period, but being considered a dangerous rival of the Guelph supporter, Florence, became its untamed rival. In 1235, Florence gained the advantage and compelled its rival to a forced peace with drastic results: Siena was stripped of her territories. Siena conformed and rebuilt its image. But the conflict was not over; Florence once more tried to gain the upper hand and, in spite of two victories beneath its walls and at Montaperti, Siena, with its allies Pisa, Pistoia and Arezzo, was defeated in 1269.

From then on, relationships with Florence changed and Siena, governed by the «Nine» (representatives of a like number of families), regained its splendour. It again underwent various rules, plagues, wars and outrages, never surrendering but always reacting with an untamed spirit until 1555, when it was forced to give in to the siege of Germans and Spaniards, finishing under the rule of Cosimo de' Medici in 1559. It remained under the Medicis for a long period until, with the rest of Tuscany, it passed to the House of Lorena.

The Risorgimento witnessed Siena in the foreground and, in 1859, it was the first city of the region to attach itself to the Kingdom of Italy. Splendid monuments and art treasures bear witness to the culture and the life of the city: the Palazzo Pubblico (Town Hall), built between 1297 and 1310 with the Torre del Mangia (bell tower) (1348); the Fonte Gaia (Fountain of Joy) (1419); the Duomo and Baptistry (1100-1376); the Merchant's House; the monumental and intact walls (seven kilometres long) with their gates: on one of these, Porta Camollia, is written the famous phrase «Cor magis tibi Siena pandit» or «Siena opens an even greater heart to you» (than this gate); St. Dominic's Church; the Chigi-Saracini Palace; Fontebranda; the St. Barbara fortress; the house of St. Catherine, etc.

As well as the Patron Saint of Italy, Siena has also had many other illustrious sons, including the sculptor Jacopo della Quercia, the painters Duccio di Boninsegna, Pietro Lorenzetti and Simone Martini, the painter and architect Baldassarre Peruzzi and the novelist Federigo Tozzi, etc.

La Fonte Gaia by Jacopo della Quercia.

Guidoriccio da Fogliano (1315), masterpiece by Simone Martini, detail of the fresco inside the Sala del Mappamondo in the Palazzo Pubblico.

PIAZZA DEL CAMPO

This square, which has always been the heart of the city, has a shape which is unique throughout the world. Situated at the confluence of the three hills on which Siena stands, it has an original scollop or fan shape, emphasized by the characteristic rosy colour of its stone flooring. Subdivided into nine «segments» which branch out in front of the Palazzo Pubblico and which are a reference to the Rule of the Nine, it is surrounded by flag-stones which provide almost a frame for the square and by a series of splendid palaces.

IL PALIO

To talk of the Piazza del Campo without mentioning the Palio is impossible. It is in fact here that twice a year, on July 2nd and August 16th, the ancient tournament of horses between the contrades (parishes) is held. Ten of the seventeen contrade into which the city is divided are chosen at random. These bear the names of Aquila, Chiocciola, Onda, Pantera, Selva, Tartuca, Civetta, Leocorno, Nicchio, Valdimonte, Torre, Bruco, Drago, Giraffa, Istrice, Lupa and Oca. And every year, tens of thousands of spectators watch this stupendous dramatic competition. The Palio is not, however, merely a show: it is the very essence of the city, which on these dates parades the ancient passions which bore witness to its fighting and untamed spirit. The great festival begins some days before the dispute with the drawing of the horses, which are then blessed together with their jockeys in the respective churches of each parish on the day of the Palio. In the morning of the race, Mass is celebrated in the Cappella di Piazza while the parish standards and the Palio itself are blessed in the church of Santa Maria di Provenzano on July 2nd and in the Cathedral on August 16th. In the afternoon the historic parade takes place, opened by the macebearers of the Commune and followed by the centurions, the representatives of the ten parishes drawn for the Palio, those of the excluded parishes and finally the Carroccio (chariot) on which the Palio (prize) is placed. While the bell in the Torre del Mangia tolls, the solemn moment of the race takes place. It lasts only a minute, the time necessary for the horses to run three times round the square with their jockeys riding bare-back and the crowd shouting encouragement. Then the triumph of the winners.

The Palio's track; The «Mossa», the start of the race; Piazza del Campo during the Palio; Glimpse of the Palazzo Pubblico.

124

THE DUOMO

More than two centuries were needed to complete the construction of the magnificent Sienese church. Begun in around 1150, it was not finished until 1376. Its foundations stand on an ancient pagan temple and, precisely because it was constructed over such a long period, it bears traces of various styles: Romanesque, Gothic, ornate Gothic. The lower part of the beautiful façade in pink Siena stone and green Prato stone is the work of Giovanni Pisano while the upper part is that of Giovanni de Cecco. The three spires contain mosaics by Castellani, of the last century. Under the central spire is a large rose-window with scenes from the Last Supper and around this are the busts of the four Evangelists and of 36 Patriarchs

and Prophets. The dome has a hexagonally shaped base. The precious paving, uncovered only from August 15th to September 15th, is one of its rarest attributes. It consists of 56 pictures and was the work of about forty artists, among whom were Matteo di Giovanni, Urbano da Cortona, Antonio Federighi, Domenico Beccafumi, Domenico di Bartolo, etc. Among the works of particular note are the statues of Bernini, a prized stained glass window designed by Duccio di Boninsegna, numerous works by Jacopo della Quercia and other famous works, among which is Nicola Pisano's wonderful pulpit. Supported by nine columns of granite, porphyry and marble (a central one and the others to hold up the octagonal base), the upper part

is divided into various panels, separated by statues of Saints and Prophets. The façades represent the Nativity, the Adoration of the Magi, the Presentation at the Temple, the Massacre of the Innocents, the Crucifixion, the Final Judgement of the Bad and the Final Judgement of the Good. The eighth façade is that of the «opening» of the access stairway.

THE DUOMO. Left: Designed by Agostino di Giovanni and Agnolo di Ventura and built in 1313, the bell tower features a horizontal black and white marble band motif matching the Duomo's, six windows which progress from a single-light to a six-light mullion window, and a pyramid-like cusp with polygonal base at the top. Above: The superb pulpit by Giovanni Pisano.

Picturesque medieval street

Palazzo dei Paschi di Siena

Via Santa Caterina, the patron saint of Italy, and her house.

The famous Fonte Branda

Above: The Abbazia (Abbey) of **Monte Oliveto Maggiore**. Situated on a wooded height suggesting solitude, it was founded by Bernardo Tolomei in 1313 and is one of Tuscany's most important treasures, not to mention the works of art it houses. Centre and below: Panorama of **Montepulciano**, including the splendid façade of the Palazzo Comunale (1300) attributed to Michelozzo. Stately in appearance and notable for its works of art in the Florentine style, it bears the seal of the Middle Ages in its layout. The town is also known for its vineyards and fine local wine.

PIENZA

Once inside the Valdorcia along the road from Montepulciano to Siena, we encounter Pienza, a scenic Tuscan village silent and solitary atop its hill overlooking the Tresa stream.

Once known as Corsignano, its name was changed to Pienza by Pope Pius II (13th August 1462) upon completion at his behest of the town's present layout which is clearly Renaissance-inspired.

Above: Palazzo Comunale and the Duomo's (1459-62) apse and bell tower.

CHIANCIANO TERME

One of the most important spas in Italy for the effectiveness of its waters in curing disorders of the liver, Chianciano Terme is just inside the southern part of the Valdichiana in an elevated open setting.

In layout, the town can be said to have a dual nature. There is the old town — perhaps Etruscan in origin — featuring narrow winding lanes and monuments within medieval walls; and the modern town comprising the spa, hotels, villas, palazzi and fashionable shops laid out along avenues set off by the lush green of parks and gardens.

Staffed by highly qualified personnel and fitted with the most modern equipment, the spa presently includes four springs, each of which has its particular properties — Acqua Santa, Acqua di Silena, Acqua di Ficoli and Acqua Sant'Elena. Known to the Etruscans, widely enjoyed by the Romans, exploited during the Commune epoch of the Middle Ages, these thermal baths have reached their full potential only recently through proper organisation and planning.

Views: The modern town and the rooms and gardens of the spa.

MONTALCINO

Settled by the Etruscans and then the Romans, this ancient town has experienced, like all the other small towns of Tuscany, the conflicts between Siennese and Florentines and the internicine strife between Guelphs and Ghibellines. Even its geographical position seems to evoke something of the waxing and waning of these events, with the town being situated on a rise dominating orderly olive groves on the one hand and wildly desolate Ombrone and Asso valleys on the other. Although mainly an agricultural centre, Montalcino also boasts shoe and clothing industries.

Below: The Palazzo Comunale (13th-14th century) and the Abbey of Sant'Antimo, an important Romanesque work of art (13th century).

131

SAN GIMIGNANO

The attraction of San Gimignano lies in the charm of its 14 towers — originally there were 72 — that soar above the town proper, the unmistakable landmarks uniquely distinguishing the medieval city.

Dominating the Elsa valley (settled by the Etruscans) with its olive groves and vineyards from its hilltop vantage, the town was originally founded on farming and trade along the ancient Via Francigena. With the rise of the communes, 12th-13th centuries, San Gimignano's main monuments begin to take form and project skyward above the same thoroughfare. This era also marks the height of the town's expansion with the addition of the San Matteo and San Giovanni districts beside the older

Left: The Collegiata or Duomo. A fine example of 12th-century Romanesque, it is located in the square or piazza of the same name. Right: Medieval tower and the Arco dei Becci which was part of the first circle of walls. Adjacent: Piazza della Cisterna with the Cisterna (1273) at the centre. The piazza is the town's centre and features a triangular plan and herring-bone-motif brick paving. Below: Scenic panorama of the Elsa valley.

fortified nucleus and the erection round them of the walls in the late 13th century (most of these walls are still preserved). Once encircled, the old city was to remain intact, impervious to the influences of Florence and Siena, both of which ruled the town at different times, as well as those of the Renaissance and neoclassicism. Unspoiled even today, it is perhaps the most engaging example of a medieval town in all Tuscany and a genuine point of interest for any visitor.

Panorama of the Piazza del Duomo, the Palazzo del Podestà and its Torre Rognosa which dominates the villages and the wide expanse of the surrounding lowlands. Above: Large vault and inner courtyard of the Palazzo del Popolo (1288), the town hall. Right: One of the town's charming streets.

135

MONTE AMIATA

The highest peak in Tuscany south of the Arno at 1738 metres above sea level, this massive, isolated cone of volcanic origin rests on a scaly clay base that by itself is 1000 metres high. It rises in the very heart of Tuscany amidst the Orcia, Fiora and Paglia valleys, a natural setting of rare beauty.

The porous nature of its rock makes the mountain a veritable fountain of natural springs, several of which are hot. These springs, which originate at an altitude ranging between 500 and 900 metres up the mountain where the villages of Abbadia San Salvadore, Castel del Piano, Piancastagnaio, Arcidosso and Santa Fiora are located, supply the aqueducts of Siena and Grosseto.

Fields of grain, olive groves and vineyards mark the foothills, chestnut stands cover the middle slopes, beech woods (including trees of remarkable size) range over the zone above 900-1000 metres (this belt bursts into perfumed colours with the May flowering of broom, strawberry, sweet violet and snowdrop), and snow caps the northern face of the summit until late spring.

Monte Amiata's past fame rested on its deposits of mercury sulphide (the cinnabar of the ancients), which had been mined since the Etruscans for its value as a dye. The mining area is a narrow 20-km belt running in a north-south direction and includes the Selvena, San Filippo, Solforate, Siele, Bagni and Abbadia San Salvadore mines which are still operating.

Steeped in the lore and culture of the region, Amiata mountain is a gift of nature that has become one of the main tourist attractions of Tuscany in both winter and summer. Its summit, topped by an imposing cross of metal trellis-work, affords the visitor an impressive panorama extending far and wide — from the Modenese Apennines and the peaks in Umbria, the Marche and Abruzzo to the Monti Cimini, the Tyrrhenian Sea and the Island of Elba.

Views: Scenic locales of Monte Amiata and the monumental trellis cross.

AREZZO

From its dominant position overlooking the Chiana, Tiber and Arno valleys, Arezzo still preserves the glories of its ancient past. One of the most powerful both militarily and industrially of the Locomonie of the Etruscan League of 12 Cities even before Rome — which would rise to conquer it — was founded, it continues to evoke the deeds and events of antiquity in the unearthed vases, bronze statues and other artifacts brought to light as in the ruins and massive walls yet surrounding the city.

Save the enduring influence of its art, Etruscan Arezzo fell to the might of Rome, under which it would rise anew to even greater heights as Roman Arezzo. By the first century BC, it had become a Roman «municipium» and its fame had spread throughout the world as the manufacturer of the highly prized coral vases artfully fashioned by its skilled craftsmen with techniques handed down from the Etruscans.

In the Middle Ages it was ruled first by the Langobards and then the Marquises of Tuscany before becoming a sovereign Commune in the 11th century. Throughout Tuscany, this period was marked by internecine city strife as by inter-city conflicts, and Arezzo was no exception. More often than not it was pitted against Florence by which it was soundly defeated in the battle of Campaldino (Casentino) in 1289. Thereafter it was ruled by a succession of local nobles and condottieri (soldiers of fortune) until being sold to Florence, under which it would remain until the unification of Italy.

Now as in the past, Arezzo is a city typified by its

works of art which have borne tangible witness to the city's history down through the ages. Today scholars and tourists come from far and wide to see its many masterpieces.

There are three key points of interest for any visit to the city: The Pieve, notable for its Romanesque architecture and polyptych by Pietro Lorenzetti, the Basilica of San Francesco with its celebrated frescoes by Pier della Francesca, and the impressive Piazza Grande.

The Basilica of San Francesco. Situated in the main city square, it is a Gothic building with Umbro-Tuscan influences of Franciscan inspiration. Begun at the end of the 13th and finally completed in the 15th century, it is a stone and brick construction (facing was applied only to the base of the façade) featuring a bell tower which was added in 1600.

The interior, consisting of a large single nave terminating in three chapels, is adorned by frescoes, among which are the magnificent «I Trionfi della Croce» (The Triumphs of the Cross), by Pier della Francesca, the church's most significant pieces.

Above: The Basilica and Piazza of San Francesco. Right: The Queen of Sheba in adoration by the bridge the wood of which became the cross of Christ.

139

Piazza Grande. Built about 1200 and incorporating changes made in the 16th century, it is a majestic and beautiful square by virtue of its irregular lay-out and the strongly contrasting architecture of different styles and periods that give it a unique character and an unusual harmony — brought into particular relief when the square becomes the multi-coloured and resplendent stage for the Giostra del Saracino (Saracen's Joust) held annually in September. Left: The Romanesque «apse» of the Pieve in the foreground; the Fontana Pubblica (Public Fountain), early 1500s, at the corner of Via Seteria; and, beyond the apse, the austere Palazzo del Tribunale (17th-18th century) right next to which is the splendid Palazzo della Fraternità dei Laici, a building erectedd over different periods and hence the result of various styles. The façade is Renaissance over Gothic superbly blended in the wealth of ornamental detail. The Pietà by Spinello can be seen in the upper lunette or tympanum of the centre door (Gothic as is the whole lower part). The upper part is wholly Renaissance and features a central bas-relief of the «Vergine della Misericordia» (Virgin of Mercy), 1460, by Giuliano and Algozzo da Settignano who also designed the balustrade and small loggia. The campanile or bell tower, 16th-century and designed by Vasari, has an ingenious clock which marks the days, the phases of the moon and the path of the sun.

The imposing 1573 Palazzo della Loggia completes the right side of the square. The southeast side features a row of medieval houses, including the tower-house of the Lappolis dating to the 14th century at No. 37. On the side facing that of Palazzo della Loggia, and closing the square, is the medieval Palazzo Cofani-Brizzolari and the 13th-century crenellated tower called the «Faggiolana».

Santa Maria della Pieve. Set atop the rise on which the Etruscan «Arretium» was founded, it is one of the finest examples in all Tuscany of Romanesque architecture. Erected in 1140 to take the place of an older church, it was completed in its present form in 1300 with the addition of certain Gothic elements.

The Romanesque façade, showing Pisan-Lucchese influences, is adorned by five blind arcades at the base with three orders of overhead loggias (arranged horizontally) formed by slender columns and arches. The 59-m high bell tower built in 1300 on the right side of the church is also called the tower of «the one-hundred holes» because of the 40 two-light mullion windows it features.

The interior, composed of a central nave and two aisles all leading to the imposing presbytery, contains a number of masterpieces from different epochs, among which the most celebrated is the polyptych depicting the Madonna and child with four saints, the Annunciation, the Assumption and twelve saints (1320) by Pietro Lorenzetti.

The Duomo. This majestic and imposing work, Gothic in origin, was designed by Margaritone, a native of Arezzo, and finally completed more than two centuries later at the beginning of the 1500s. It thus reflects changes in style during this period, among which are the differences between the lower and upper arcades, and the Romanesque combined with the oval motif of the large double windows. The statues of the façade and the sculpted bas-reliefs in the lunettes of the portals are by Giuseppe Cassioli and Enrico Quattrini.

The enormous interior features a nave and aisles separated by pillars of various styles and oval arches setting off masterpieces of art, among which is the superb fresco of «La Maddalena» (1465) by Pier della Francesca (left).

141

Santa Maria delle Grazie. The church was begun in 1445 to replace a chapel that St Bernard had ordered erectedd in 1428 following the destruction of the pagan shrine called the Fonte Tecla. The superbly elaborate portico, with its seven front arcs and two on each side supported by slender Corinthian columns, was designed by Benedetto da Maiano and built towards the end of 1440. The interior, with its simple nave and groin vault, contains many valuable works of art, the most important of which is the masterpiece, on the high altar, in marble and terra cotta (1500s) by Andrea della Robbia.

The Roman Amphitheatre. Built between the late first and early second century AD of sandstone and brick, it has an elliptical form featuring two tiers of seats (the shorter 68 metres and the longer 121 metres).

The Giostra del Saracino. Celebrated since 1593 but dating in origin to the 1200s, the joust is held every year on the first Sunday in September in Piazza Grande. A magnificent spectacle in costume, it is enacted by 8 knights representing Arezzo's eight original city districts. Mounted on their colourful steeds and with lance at the ready, they charge one at a time an armoured, swivel-action dummy called the «Saracino» which is armed with a whip and shield. A point is scored each time a knight strikes the Saracino's shield with his lance and avoids being hit by the whip. The winner is the knight with the most points at the end of the joust.

142

CORTONA

Situated on the upper slope of a mountain area known as Sant'Egidio at the point in which the Valdichiana and the Tiber valley converge, the town itself, largely built of sandstone, is erected on a sheer spur or buttress and enclosed by a vast network of Etruscan walls which link up with Girifalco, the fortress of the Medicis. Here at Cortona Etruscan civilisation is still vitally important.

Its most important works of art were executed before and during the Commune period (12th-13th centuries) when the guilds of artists and craftsmen were at their most active. The most important monuments include the Palazzo Comunale (1241), Palazzo Pretorio (1200) and churches like San Francesco (1245). During Florentine domination in the Renaissance, new buildings such as the church of the Madonna del Calcinaio (1458) designed by Francesco di Giorgio Martini and Palazzo Mancini-Sernini (1533) by Cristofanello were added. The Medici influence was again to be felt after the mid-1500s in the person of Cosimo I who provided new stimulus for both military projects — the Medici fortress of Girifalco (1549) — and additional civic projects designed to enrich the artistic

and architectural fabric of the town. The Medici rule also brought about a substantial cultural flowering from 1440-1600.

Today another dramatic awakening is taking place. The town is now committed to preserving its old city, to promoting a tourism emphasising its historical, artistic and environmental resources and values and to developing an antiques trade.

Views: The Palazzo del Comune; Scenic panorama of the Valdichiana from the ancient walls; The so-called «Tanella di Pitagora» (Pythagoras' Den), 4th-1st century B.C., famous hypogeum or Etruscan burial chamber; The Madonna del Calcinaio (1485), superb Renaissance church designed by Francesco di Giorgio Martini, and «the Annunciation» by Beato Angelico.

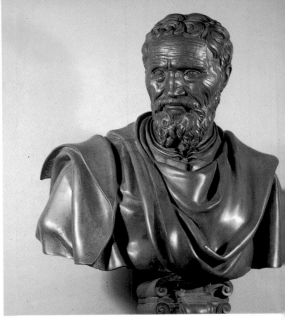

CAPRESE MICHELANGELO

This farming community atop a rugged hill dominating the Valle del Sigerna is the birthplace of Michelangelo Buonarroti, painter, sculptor, architect and poet. One of the greatest artists of history, he was also a man of great humanity. A few words in his honour would certainly not be amiss.

Born on March 6th 1475, Michelangelo symbolised more than any other man or artist the new idea of man with which, through his studies of the classics, he had helped to imbue the Italian Renaissance. That concept, forget amid the strife and conflict of the times, strove to celebrate the individual by setting man at the centre of the universe and portraying him as a being at once sublime, creative, heroic, and vigorous — the focal point of reality, the protagonist of history and life itself in sharp contrast to the thought of the Middle Ages.

His numerous works are to be found in Florence, Rome and Bologna (sculptures of his youth in the church of San Domenico). Those which are most representative of his driving force, those that bear his message to humanity, are the «Pietà» in St Peter's Basilica (which represents the end of his first phase of study) and the frescoes of the vault and walls, including the Last Judgement, on the Sistine Chapel.

Completed in 1541, these frescoes are the fruit of Michelangelo's maturity, and in them are to be found the first signs of a crisis — a crisis no longer latent involving the ideals of the Renaissance. It will lead him to eschew his faith in man as in himself. It is the crisis that will torment him in every endeavour to the hour of his death, which will come for him in Rome in 1564.

Above: The birthplace and a portrait of the artist. Left: Details of the Pietà and frescoes of the Sistine Chapel.

CASENTINO

Tuscany's Casentino is a zone of fertile cultivated valleys and elevations set against the scenic grandeur of the tree-covered Apennine foothills. The picturesque towns and villages scattered throughout still preserve intact their medieval architectural legacy and their unique historical traditions. The Casentino is associated with Dante, St Francis of Assisi (who received the Stigmata while in retreat on Monte della Verna), St Romuald (who founded his hermitage at Camaldoli), the famous medieval Pieve di Romena, and the numerous masterpieces by the della Robbias. Many of the valley's villages offer the natural calm and quiet of scenic ambience in an ideal setting for a relaxing summer holiday.

Left: The Castello dei Conti Guidi (12th century) at Poppi. Above: The Santuario (shrine) della Verna with the church of Santa Maria degli Angeli (13th century). Below: Panorama of the Hermitage of Camaldoli.

GROSSETO

Lying on a flat to the right of the Ombrone river, it can be called the natural capital of the Maremma. It lies along the road of the same name that stretches from Pisa to Rome and is a short 12 Kms from the sea.

Grosseto has expanded well beyond the walls enclosing its old medieval centre and is today a dynamic, thriving farm product and livestock business town important for its processing industries (wine, seed oils, dairy and grain mills).

Its growth in the Middle Ages coincided with the decline, or rather demise in the wake of Saracen raiders in 935 of the neighbouring Etruscan city of Roselle, which was forced to transfer its civic institutions and activities — including the archbishopric later to be the see of Pope Innocent II in 1138 — to Grosseto.

Fief of the Aldobrandeschi family from the 11th century, Grosseto was subsequently ruled by the Sienese from 1336 to 1559, when it fell under the power of the Medicis. It grew rapidly under Florentine stewardship, especially during the epoch of Francesco I who had its walls erectedd in 1574 and fostered various renovations and land reclamation projects. Grosseto today is a thriving town with a thriving economy that, in addition to its farm commodities and food processing, is reaping the benefits of an expanded tourism along the coast as well as in the interior's national park.

The high points of any visit should include the walls with their hexagon bastions, the Medici fortress and the town's medieval centre, the Romanesque Duomo (1294-1302), the Gothic church of San Francesco (13th century), the Museo Diocesano di Arte Sacra (Diocesan Museum of Sacred Art) and the Archaeological Museum.

Above left: The Palazzo della Provincia at Piazza Dante. Left: The Duomo. Adjacent: Etruscan vases in the Archaeological Museum. Above: Church of San Francesco. Below: The Medici Fortress. Right: The Madonna dell'Uccellino by Pietro Lorenzetti in the Diocesan Museum of Sacred Art. Below: The Monument to Leopold II and Etruscan vase from Roselle.

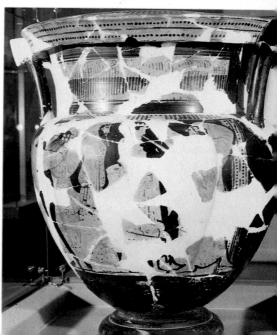

LA MAREMMA

Originally an infested area of swamps and marshlands as popular folk songs and ballads attest, the Maremma today, thanks to land reclamation projects and agrarian reform, is a fertile agro-industrial zone with a growing economic base which has received a sharp boost from the tourist industry along the coast and the forward-looking management of its national parks.

Among them is the splendid preserve set aside as a national park — an area made up of a small chain of tree-covered hills, 15 kms long and 4-5 kms wide, culminating in Poggio dei Lecci — known as the **MONTI DELL'UCCELLINA** hills.

Running parallel to the coast, these hills drop into the sea as outcroppings. The Torre dell'Uccellina (347 m high) and the Torre della Bella Marsilia (232 m high) on the ridge once formed, along with the Collelungo, Cala di Forno, delle Cannelle and Capo d'Uomo coastal towers, a defensive system of lookout posts connected to the forts at Castiglione della Pescaia and Talamone.

148

FROM FOLLONICA TO TALAMONE

The stretch of coast road running from Follonica to Marina di Grosseto and Talamone — about 70 Kms — offers the traveler a truly splendid landscape of superb natural beauty. Across broad swaths of pines and up rises with panoramic views of the Tuscan archipelago, the road slopes down towards the promontory of **Punta Ala**, wedged out into the sea with its beach. Of striking beauty, it is also all you could want of the most modern seaside resort — fashionable summer flats, luxury hotels, well-appointed shops, golf course, tennis courts, polo field, riding school, swimming pools and, of course, fashionable night spots.

A bit farther along our route are the splendid pine stand of Castiglione, with its camping and motor home and trailer facilities, and **Castiglione della Pescaia**, the most famous, stylish and modern seaside resort of the Tuscan Maremma. From here, it is but a short drive (11 Kms) over coastal hills and through woods and pine stands — punctuated here and there by balcony-like vistas of the sea — to **Marina di Grosseto**. Set in the middle of the beach stretching between the promontory of Castiglione della Pescaia in the north and the Ombrone river in the south, it is a very fine resort beach,

with excellent facilities, that keeps growing. Nothing typifies the town more than its charming rustic villas hemmed in by green and lining the streets behind the beautiful beach.

Before coming to Talamone, we cross the Ombrone and find ourselves among the splendid hills of the Monti dell'Uccellina, gateway to our destination. A fishing village partly reconstructed after the Second World War, **Talamone** is a growing beach town dominated by the imposing remains of its medieval castle.

Left: Castiglione della Pescaia, Punta Ala and Talamone.

149

ARGENTARIO

Hilly promontory on the Tuscan coast, it is linked to the mainland by two sand cordons called «tomboli» (literally pillow-laces) which embrace the Orbetello lagoon, spread out and culminate in the 635-metre high Monte Telegrafo. Its settlement can be traced as far back as the Etruscans and includes the Greeks, Romans, Spanish, Bourbons, and, in annexation to the Grand Duchy of Tuscany, the Tuscans. During their rule in the 17th century, the Spaniards erectedd a gigantic fortress, effectively

Left: The Duomo of Orbetello, 1376. Dedicated to Our Lady of the Assumption, it features a Gothic façade in travertine marble of golden reflection.

turning Argentario into a base of operations for a fleet of numerous merchant sailing ships which plied the trade routes in the mid- and upper Tyrrhenian.

There is a scenic road running along its perimeter which affords some spectacular views of the changing landscape — panoramic vistas of the rocky coast with its narrow, winding depressions and the unending hillside terraces of vineyards and orchards of every kind crowned by the hilltop woodlands, not to mention the small charming villas and picturesque hamlets dotting nature's intricate pattern. Although forest fires destroyed almost 60% of the vegetation in 1981, its natural beauty has remained intact.

Trade, tourism and fishing are the staples of life, with Porto Santo Stefano and Porto Ercole — the two largest towns — being the centres of most activity.

PORTO SANTO STEFANO (above right). Situated between the beach and the rising hills behind, it is the seat of the township of Argentario and an important commercial fishing harbour. It has an intense tourist activity in the summer months both as a resort in itself with its excellent beach and as the embarkation point for the Giglio and Giannutri islands.

PORTO ERCOLE (below right). An open and inviting village built on sand-carpeted shoreline along the eastern side of the promontory, it is dominated by the La Rocca and San Filippo forts built during the reign of the Spanish king Philip IV. Porto Ercole, with its multi-coloured fishermen's dwellings, is an important fishing and beach locale.

151

THE ISOLA DEL GIGLIO

Second island in size after Elba of the Tuscan archipelago, Giglio (lily) is a mere 14 Kms from Argentario. Elliptical in shape and granite in formation, it is a rocky display of irregular coast and offshore outcroppings just right for spear fishing. In addition to its Mediterranean climate (so mild it never drops below 0°C, 32°F) and vegetation, the island's resources include wine grapes, olives, fishing and the natural amenities conducive to a growing tourism.

There are three towns on the island. **GIGLIO PORTO** (above), set on a beautiful broad sandy beach along the eastern shore, lies beneath the balcony-like vineyards of the foothills. **CAMPESE** (centre) is a splendid village overlooking a magnificent gulf featuring a long sandy ribbon of beach — the most accommodating on the island — and boasts extensive resort facilities. At one end of the gulf rises Torre Campese, built during the reign of Ferdinand I of Spain. And **GIGLIO CASTELLO** (below), built on a 405-metre hilltop at the island's centre.

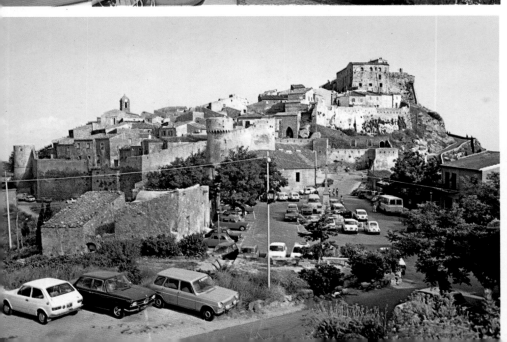

SOVANA

As one's breath seems to hover above the syllables in pronouncing its name, so time seems to have all but stopped in the remote past for this once-proud medieval city. Semi-abandoned today, Sovana has fallen in discreet toppling to partial ruin, the architecture and spatial patterns of which have conspired to create a striking metaphysical presence.

Its modern avatar belies its glorious past — first under the Etruscans from the 7th and 6th centuries B.C., and then under the Romans from the 3rd century B.C. onwards. The onset of decline began with the rule of the Orsini family in the 14th century, followed by a series of wars and malaria epidemics that were to thwart even the stubborn efforts at renewal promoted by the Grand Duchy of Tuscany and the Lorena family. Sovana is also noted as the birthplace of the celebrated pope Gregory VII (1020-85).

Above: Duomo of San Pietro and San Paolo (12th-13th century), built on a pre-existant structure dating to the 9th-11th centuries, and Piazza del Pretorio, centre of the old town.

MASSA MARITTIMA

Across the expanse of the Mucini flood plain the road runs up into the hills and enters the town, notable for its well preserved medieval core concentrated in Piazza Garibaldi. Massa is really two towns — the «old» centre below and the «new» one above. Its first period of splendour is linked to the power of the clergy, when the episcopal see is transferred here from Populonia in the 9th century, and then to the rise of the Communes, when it was called the Republic of Massetana (1225) and the skilled crafting and trading of metal is at its apex.

This latter era coincided with, or rather was marked by the renewal of the old town and the lay out of a new street plan in response to the demands for expansion of the emerging bourgeoisie (13th-14th centuries), whose interests centred on the mining and metal working industries which have always formed, along with agriculture, the economic base of Massa Marittima.

Below: Town panorama and the Duomo, a fine example of early 13th-century Romanesque-Gothic.

ETRUSCAN ITINERARIES

The Region of Tuscany has undertaken to public acclaim a series of highly successful cultural exhibitions and initiatives showcasing the Etruscans. It is a subject — their life, society and relations with the Italic people, Greeks and Phoenicians — that inevitably conjures up that aura of mystery in which it has always been shrouded. The fascination stems in all likelihood from the legendary tales recorded in traditional historical sources, or perhaps from writings of the Greeks, which were little more than thinly disguised propaganda of a naive turn, bent on lending credence to those legends or tales by recounting the amoral nature of the Etruscans whom, as their bitter rivals, the Greeks tried to discredit by every means at hand.

This aura of mystery is exploited today, too. Every time a necropolis is discovered, speculation as to the tumuli (mortuary mounds) and artifacts runs rampant, often reaching the spectacular, and the old legends are again in the public eye. Science and archaeology, however, have been successful in separating fact from fiction and have largely consigned the centuries-old legends to their rightful place in folklore and literary embellishment. These efforts have enormously increased our knowledge of this ancient people in the last few decades. The data these studies have yielded have even provided the analytic and comparative tools necessary to piece together a complete picture of the Etruscan language, the last great puzzle remaining.

These advances were made possible by a shift in emphasis. Researchers began to turn their attention from the necropolis to historical reconstruction and social organisation. Archaeologists began setting their sights on aspects which had hitherto remained neglected such as Etruscan settlements, urban areas, shrine or temple precincts, manufactory complexes and ports. Though less gratifying and spectacular than the unearthing of necrop-

Etruscan funerary lion's head .(5th century BC) from Bolsena. Florence's Museo Archeologico. Below: Villanova funeral urn (8th century BC), Florence Archaeological Museum; gold buckle from Vetulonia necropolis.

olises and tombs, the archaeological diggings and research efforts over the last 20-30 years, with the emphasis on urban centres and settlements, has led to a detailed reconstruction of the genesis and development of the city in particular, and Etruria in general, as well as the relations of the Etruscans themselves with other peoples.

This approach has been rewarded by the discovery of artifacts which have greatly added to our knowledge and have even greater import for the historical record. Among the most notable are the double-edged gold blades of Etruscan-phoenician manufacture at Pirgy, the ports of Caere (Cerveteri) and Gravisca, and the port of Tarquinia, a discovery which enabled Etruria's most important trade centres to be identified. Populonia was found to be a centre of metallurgy with links to a similar site on the island of Elba. Together with the excavations of Roselle, Tarquinia, Spina and others locations, these findings and those of the necropolises made it possible to restore the mosaic of an age that had been lost to time. The data also yielded a profile of the society — the social fabric, the role of women, customs, religious beliefs and economic activity in the fields of agriculture, manufacturing and trade.

Current historical research supports the view that Etruscan society was largely based on two classes — a distinction which becomes more pronounced after the pe-

riod of the Villanova culture with the advent of eastern influences from the 7th to the 5th centuries B.C. The dominant class is that of the «princes» or «leaders», the wealthy who hold the reins of power. The second class was subordinate to the ruling elite. Known as «servants», they comprised the greater part of the people and were divided mainly into two groups: those who worked in the homes of the aristocracy serving as domestics in general, in the personal service of the lords as anything from cup-bearers to musicians at formal banquets, and as house-hold and personal handmaids to the mistress of the man-or; and the peasants, by far the most numerous category, who were not unlike serfs. They provided the labour on the vast country or agricultural estates of the «princes» on whom they were personally dependent. The members of this subaltern class were rigidly excluded from any form of power whatsoever and forbidden to contract marriage with women of the ruling class. The wealth and «opulent» luxury of the power-wielding elite was founded on the exploitation of the servants.

The role or status of the Etruscan woman in the ar-chaic and classical ages was different indeed from that of her Greek and Roman counterparts. The archaeological evidence from the Villanova culture shows that the wom-an is still closely identified with the hearth and domestic activities. Individual tombs are the norm and the classes are as yet undifferentiated. Women were buried with spindles and spools, linking them with spinning and weav-ing, and a few simple ornamental objects, mainly bronze brooches. Towards the end of the 8th century, however, important changes begin to appear. The objects accompa-nying the dead in some of the tombs become more valu-able, a sign that wealth is increasing, but only among a select few. The burial sites and the artifacts in them clearly show the difference between the aristocracy and the lower classes.

The tombs of the governing class were meant to dis-play all the pomp and circumstance that had accompan-ied their occupants in life. They were well appointed as only befits the final resting place of the progenitors of the Etruscan elite, with the wife or consort being laid out next «her» lord and surrounded by objects both personal and symbolic of that social rank. Successive generations will even be interred in the same chamber as proof of an-cestral lineage — death is the *raison d'etre* of the ruling nobility and the instrument by which its power is legiti-mised.

Internally designed to faithfully render the life of the deceased, the tumulus is the source of what we know about the particular role of the Etruscan woman within the family and in society, especially in the age dominated by eastern influences. Unlike Greek and Roman women who were tradition-bound to fulfill their roles inside the home, Etruscan women were to a certain extent «free» to engage actively in the various forms of public and private life. There are numerous examples in Etruscan art of this freedom where women are depicted attired in richly orna-mented dress and heavy wraps or cloaks as they watch contests, dances, gymnastics and gladiatorial combats.

From above: Pediment from Talamone in Florence Archaeologi-cal Museum; so-called «Crater of the Argonauts» in Florence Ar-chaeological Museum; Plikasna silver «situla» from Chiusi.

There are also epigraphic inscriptions in which the names of the father and mother of the person to whom the epigraph is dedicated appear side by side, a fact which occurs all too frequently for it to be considered a simple act of affection. It needs be kept in mind, however, that such a privileged situation was extended only to the Etruscan women of the ruling nobility and courtesans. In other words, the «freer» social standing and legal status of these women were due to distinct social and economic factors designed to ensure the continuity of wealth and lineage. Initially dynamic, the role of women becomes rigidly fixed in the hierarchical Etruscan social structure through time and falls prey to a slow but inexorable decline.

Religious beliefs and practices were another important facet of Etruscan life, one that attracted keen interest even among writers of antiquity. The Etruscans were so imbued with the religious spirit that their rites of worship attained such a degree of formality as to border on obsession, a fact which was duly noted by historians. One of the main tenets of their system was fate, a concept practically unknown until then. From it stems the anxiety connected with knowing the will of the gods as made manifest through the heavenly bodies, the entrails of sacrificed animals, lightening bolts, the flight of birds, omens and dreams. In a word, divination.

Tradition has it that the system of beliefs and divinatory practices were imparted by the demigod Tagetes, son of Genius and grandson of Jupiter, and collected in several books, which unfortunately have not come down to us. According to legend, Tagetes, who sprang from a furrow made by a peasant's plough in Tarquinia, bade the people of Etruria to assemble before him and then dictated the precepts of the new religion (the Romans called this doctrine «Etrusca Disciplina»). These teachings undoubtedly represent a synthesis of centuries-old traditions, and their setting down in written form probably dates to the founding of the «League of 12 Cities» (c. 600 B.C.). It is in fact to these cities that Tagetes appears to address his message. Predicated on the basis of general consensus, these articles were most likely seen as the most suitable means of ensuring the maximum unity and cohesion among the League's members, the task of which was to forge a national spirit (so much the more desired so much the less it was enacted).

The «Etrusca Disciplina» explained the relationship between the gods and men, the pantheon, the gods, the forms and positions of the heavenly bodies and the earth, the lifetime of man and of cities, the world beyond the grave, religious ceremonies and government. Various aspects of Etruscan religion, most notably in regard to the gods and the rites of the dead, are strikingly similar to that of the Greeks and Romans. Along with other peoples, the Etruscans believed in an afterlife, a destination that was to be safeguarded in the very burial chamber itself. This provided the fertile ground from which sprang the cult of the dead with its complex funeral rites, e.g. elaborately decorated monumental tombs embellished with furnishings, food and arms.

The features of Etruscan society we have been discussing must also be seen in relation to trade. A highly dynamic force, it shaped and propelled their striving for wealth and the development of their civilisation. The initial impetus toward their commercial exploits derived

Alabaster funeral urn with Etruscan inscriptions in Florence Archaeological Museum.

from the very land the Etruscans had settled, one of Western Europe's richest areas of ore deposits. This enabled the Etruscans to establish trade ties with other peoples on a different competitive footing, as occurred with the Italic people. Although their arrival in Etruria certainly had a lasting impact, the Greeks and Phoenicians encountered an already highly developed and organised society. Indeed, that very contact was to spur an even more rapid development than could have otherwise been expected.

Trade, too, began to reach remarkable proportions. The social fabric within the Etruscan cities underwent new alignments as production capacity increased to meet the challenge posed by the Greeks and Phoenicians. Trade expanded rapidly, setting in motion the forces of social mobility. This rise to wealth and the concomitant attraction that Etruria's cities aroused in Greece and the Ionian city-states gave impetus to another kind of movement. Merchants, artists and craftsmen began to arrive and settle in Etruria, imparting to things Etruscan a distinctive eastern style that was to distinguish subsequent artistic developments.

The Tyrrhenian coastal area soon underwent a transformation. The volume and value of the flourishing seaborne trade turned the original settlements into thriving port cities of respectable size, a rise to prominence which was marked, if not occasioned, by the fleets. Manned by experienced sailors and able men-at-arms, they made Etruscan sea power the equal of Greece's and Phoenicia's in the struggle for the dominion of the Mediterranean trade routes throughout the 6th and 5th centuries B.C.

Etruria's trade was a multi-faceted enterprise in its own right, with the quality and quantity of its goods reflected in the diversity of factors that made up the Etruscan world. The primary foreign exchange commodity, metal work, was closely seconded by the exports of olive oil and wine — produced in abundance by the countryside — to southern France. These goods were the backbone of Etruscan trade and provided the stimulus leading to the social, economic and manufacturing changes in her expanding cities. New shipyards were appointed to build the ships needed to transport these bulk commodities and new industries were established to manufacture the large black-clay (buccaro) amphorae used as containers for the oil and wine on their outbound journeys.

These innovative forces also had their effect on the entrenched aristocratic oligarchy. New vested interest

Ivory comb and mirror handle from Marsiliana (Grosseto).

changes that left a distinctive mark on the shaping and future development of the people whom today we call by the name Etruscan.

From such a vantage point the question as to the origins of the Etruscans makes little sense, or better still, pales to insignificance beside other intriguing and as yet unanswered issues awaiting archaeology in its pursuit of the Etruscans and their history.

The Etruscans in Tuscany: 5 excursions

Etruscan Tuscany is a rare world within other worlds. Together with the treasures of the Middle Ages and the Renaissance, the 5 excursions set out below afford the visitor a unique look at the art and history of one of civilisation's most important and enigmatic cultures.

1. Firenze - Fiesole — FLORENCE. The first stop is Via della Colonna 36, the city's fine Museo Archeologico. Among the museum's excellent, chronologically arranged exhibits is the exemplary collection of Etruscan artifacts and objects of art. Although many are the outstanding pieces, several are worth particular mention: the famous «Cratere François», discovered in a tomb at Chiusi, on the ground floor; the «sarcofago dell'obese» (obese man's sarcophagous) on the first floor; and the celebrated «Chimera d'Arezzo», a 4th-century bronze of exceptional value, on the second floor. FIESOLE. It is on a hilltop only a short distance from Florence along a road lined with beautiful villas. The town itself was an important Etruscan city, as the two kilometres of ancient walls testify. The sites of archaeological interest include a «tempietto» or small temple, the «baths», theatre and the museum.

2. Volterra (Velathri) — The best way to take in the Etruscan sights here is to start from the Acropolis area, clearly visible from the street named Viale dei Ponti (paved with slabs laid by the Etruscans) and the large square enclosing two temples, next which is the large Roman bathing pool.

If we begin to follow the old walls (7 kms) from here, we shall

groups began to emerge in its ranks and compete with the traditional power brokers who were still identified with metal working. The urban element was to gain the upperhand over the rural, a process which pitted city against country estate and led to Etruria's final act of development and her eventual downfall. A development which can be summed up in a word. Expansionism.

The Etruscan cities were not a unified state in which events are shaped by a common national consciousness. From the mid-7th to the early 5th century B.C., each city-state pursued its own foreign policy, reaping as it sowed. This lack of a united front would turn the triumph of expansion into the slow yet inevitable decline and final defeat at the young but powerful hands of an emerging Rome (265 B.C.).

About the only thing that can be said with any certainty is that the Etruscans probably migrated from east central Europe-Asia Minor and that their cultural evolution bears the imprint of the Bronze and Iron Ages. It must be kept in mind too that, as with the settlements, these were far from isolated developments devoid of outside contact but were events that occurred against a background of a native population in a process of assimilation and acculturation. Subsequent contact with the Greeks and Phoenicians was to initiate cultural and social

Bronze Etruscan Chimera from Arezzo, Florence Archaeological Museum.

The Pietrera, Etruscan tumulus, and perimeter walls, Roselle (Grosseto).

come to our next stop, the «Porta dell'Arco». The most important remnant of the town from the Etruscan period, it is a round arch built of stone in which are sculpted the heads of three guardian divinities. Below the arch is the first-century AD Roman theatre.

No visit to Volterra would be complete without a stop at the Museo Etrusco Guarnacci in Via Don Minzoni 15. It is justly famous for its wealth and quality of the sculpture collection (cremation urns in tufa, alabaster and terra cotta from the 6th-1st centuries BC) and the jewelry and bronze collections (among which is the so-called «ombra della sera», literally night-shadow).

3. Arezzo - Cortona - Chiusi — AREZZO. It was one of Etruria's preeminent industrial and farming centres, a fact which is borne out by the walls of the period (4th century BC) which still ring the city as well as by the valuable collection of arms, helmets, and bronze statuettes housed in the Museo Archeologico Mecenate, a 16th-century palazzo and former convent of the Olivetani religious order, in Via Margaritone 12. To the left of the museum is the Roman Amphitheatre (1st-2nd century AD), not to be missed. CORTONA. Dominating the panorama of the Val di Chiana, Cortona is also an important centre of medieval and Renaissance works of art. Apart from the city's walls and tombs, the remainder of the Etruscan artifacts are on display in the Museo dell'Accademia Etrusca located in the Palazzo Pretorio in Piazza Signorelli. The collection includes coins and votive bronzes as well as the famous bronze chandelier with sixteen spouts shaped in the image of Silenius-like figures and flute-playing sirens. CHIUSI. The road from Cortona to Chiusi passes by Lake Trasimeno, the perfect place for a brief stop. There are several points of Etruscan interest in Chiusi. The Tomba della Pellegrina, once the property of the Sentinate family, is a tomb containing numerous epigraphs sculpted on the urns of ashes; then there is

Tumulo del Diavolino (Little Devil's Tumulus) and town street, Vetulonia (Grosseto).

the visit to the Labyrinth di Cunicoli or underground passages below the old city centre which is also the basis of the legend of Porsenna's treasure; and in conclusion a visit to the Museo Nazionale Etrusco, a must. Located in Piazza del Duomo, the National Etruscan Museum is famous for its «canopi» collection (funeral urns with covers in the form of human heads) as well as ceramics and other artifacts unearthed in the local excavations.

4. Grosseto - Roselle - Vetulonia - Populonia — The Museo Archeologico della Maremma, Palazzo del Liceo, Via Mazzini 36, in Grosseto serves as the main point of reference for the coastal sites of Etruria. The entire ground floor, for example, is dedicated to artifacts found at Roselle, a hilltop town 5 kms away. The road leading to it is flanked by a series of small chamber tombs (tombe a camera); the perimeter walls are intact and the town contains the ruins of a portico and basilica.

We now return to Grosseto and, taking the Via Aurelia, head northwest towards Vetulonia, 25 Kms away. Just before entering the town is a sign indicating the Necropoli where several large tumuli can be visited. The most interesting are the Tumulo di Pietrera, a grandiose structure that recalls in its roof the domed tombs of Mycene, and the Tumulo del Diavolino (little devil), one of the best examples of Etruscan tomb architecture. A more thorough knowledge of the town's Etruscan heritage is possible by visiting the Antiquarium, in which are displayed together the oldest artifacts of the old collection and those unearthed in recent excavations.

Populonia is a short drive (35-40 kms) away. The Museo Etrusco is housed in a building called the Villa along the town's main thoroughfare and contains objects found in the local archaeological digs. The ancient city is represented by the Pozzo di Santa Caterina (St Catherine's Well) and the ruins of the Acropolis' walls. The necropolis is below the actual town, at Baratti, the Etruscan port. The site offers quite a few tombs, the most important of which are the Tomba dei Flabelli and the famous Tomba dei Carri.

5. Sovana - Pitigliano - Sorano — Although the triangle they form is not very large in area, these towns have a large number of artifacts, with Sovana heading the list. Set against the backdrop of the town's medieval core and the impressions it evokes in the eye of the beholder, the Necropoli Etrusca is a must, with its chamber tombs cut into the walls of the Fosso Calesina and the streams flowing into it. The main group can be dated to the 4th-3rd century BC and is important for the decorative motifs adorning the individual tombs. The most important for the visitor are the Sileno, Sirena, Ildebranda, the so-called Grotta Pola and the Tifone tombs, of which the Ildebranda is particularly outstanding as a replica of exceptional size of a temple with six front and four columns per side (an excellent example of Hellenistic culture's finest architectural forms).

Nine Kms to the south is Pitigliano, with the ruins of the Etruscan walls in the Porta di Sovana town gate and the Stantonia ruins (necropolis with simple and loculus or urn niche tombs) but a short distance from the town.

Sorano features the «colombari», cubicles with niches for the ashes of the deceased, and the Grotte di San Giglio, cave dwellings.

TABLE OF CONTENTS

Graphic Design and Editing: Federico Frassinetti - Bologna

Photography: Fotografia Editoriale Gaetano Barone - Florence
Renzo Santori - Lucca
Ghilardi - Lucca
Cartolibreria Turchini - Arezzo
Foto Studio M. Zilianti - Abbadia S. Salvatore (Siena)

© Copyright   LA FOTOMETALGRAFICA EMILIANA
All Rights Reserved.
Any reproduction, even in part, prohibited

Printed by: LA FOTOMETALGRAFICA EMILIANA
S. Lazzaro di Savena (Bologna) - Italy